Estate Planning *is about more than* Death & Taxes

by Cory C. Grant

ISBN 0-9759623-0-2

Library of Congress Control Number
2004110381

Printed in Canada

Published by
Westhem Grant, LLC
Solana Beach, California 92075
(858) 350-4000

Production Supervisor: Sue Joyce
Design & Production: Creative Fusion, Inc.

TABLE OF CONTENTS

"This book offers basic and in-depth discussion of proven strategies that can be used to reduce income, capital gain, and transfer taxes."

– Cal Kirby, author of Business Battle Plan

"In this groundbreaking new book you will discover the potential pitfalls of estate taxes, retirement planning, wills, trusts and other vehicles – and how to avoid them."

– Peter Ramsaroop, author of Surfing the Leadership Wave

"This is more than just a book on estate planning; this is your complete, one-stop resource for all your questions and concerns about estate and retirement planning."

– Dr. David Schumacher, author of Buy and Hold

"Understanding the many different vehicles for planning your estate is critical to making the right decisions for your assets, your family and your business. This fascinating book is filled with excellent reasons why you should plan your estate now!"

– Marsha Haigh Arend, author of I'd Rather Manage Myself

"In this book, author Cory Grant has outlined some of the most common and most important estate planning techniques, in an easy-to-understand, straightforward way to help you make those critical estate planning decisions."

– David Bradley, author of Management by Essay

ACKNOWLEDGEMENTS

I have been fortunate to have come into contact with some very interesting and intelligent people who have all, in their own way, helped me evolve and grow as a person and as an adviser. The evolution of understanding the intricacies of human nature is a complex and continuing process, and we never stop learning. I would like to thank some of these people who have contributed more to this book than they may understand.

To my partner in Westhem Grant, Andrew Westhem for being a sounding board and "guinea pig" of sorts. A great number of the estate planning strategies described in this book have been tested on Andrew and his family. To my associates and staff at Westhem Grant, I appreciate your continuing support and your ability to work with two principals with different temperaments, talents and convictions to create an awesome organization.

To my friends at the volleyball courts at 21st Street in Del Mar for helping me keep a balance in life, and giving me an excuse to get out of the office every now and again.

To my advisory board, who through their combined experience provide me with invaluable insight, diverse perspectives, and give me a "cheat sheet to life." It is a great honor to have people who have achieved significant success believe in and take an interest in you and your success. I feel the truest measure of success is when a client becomes a friend, and I am lucky to have that in all of you.

To my clients in Florida who make going to my office there feel like coming home. Your hospitality and good nature have been an integral part of my ability to grow the business in a location away from home. I appreciate you all and your willingness to provide support and make my visits to the East more enjoyable.

Finally and most importantly, to my beautiful wife Emily. You are the love of my life, my partner, confidant and friend. I love and appreciate you and your being more than I could ever express. After almost twelve years, every day with you just gets better and better. Thank you for your undying support, your uncanny insight into people and situations, and your tolerance for my idiosyncrasies. I could never have come this far without your unwavering support. I think it is because of you the phrase "behind every successful man is a good woman" was coined. You are truly special, and give me the motivation and will to be a better person every day.

A special thanks to Don Korn, Sue Joyce and Michelle Barlow for all of their diligent work in making this book a reality.

INTRODUCTION

When a friend asked what my new book would be called I responded, "Estate planning is about more than death and taxes." After looking at me in a sort of quizzical, puzzled way, he asked me, "What does that mean?" His question provoked me to think about how to respond to him and also on a much grander scale, it caused me to think about how clients perceive the estate planning process and the tax and non-tax issues associated with it.

That question turned out to be one of the most important questions anyone ever asked me. It made me rethink how this book should be presented, and gave me valuable insight into how someone who is not an estate planner views the issue.

This book is divided into two primary sections. The first is an explanation of the way wealth protection and tax reduction motivate and often drive estate planning and includes strategies and techniques commonly utilized in the estate planning process. The second part, as the title implies, utilizes case studies based on actual client's situations. Tax and non-tax issues are interwoven and must be considered in comprehensive solutions for each circumstance. The purpose of this is to provide a practical example of how some of the concepts described in the first eleven chapters can be applied to an actual family circumstance.

I have found over the past twelve years that the estate planning process is often dynamic and can be a learning experience for all those involved. The client often focuses on tax reduction and wealth protection strategies. This is often a new way of thinking as they are also learning how to shift from the accumulation phase of life into one of protection and retention, and ultimately the transfer of one's wealth to intended beneficiaries. These individuals will often consider how they may incorporate their values as an integral part of their estate plan. Understanding their motivation and specific goals often becomes a learning experience for me. It reinforces my belief that individuals who are able to achieve success in a particular field have often done so because they possess unique qualities that allow them to digest information on a particular subject that may be foreign to them and execute those pieces of information integral to the solution that they are seeking. They do this not based on familiarity with the subject matter but based on an almost innate ability to ascertain the optimum solution.

As I learn how behaviors affect one's decision-making process, I learn a tremendous amount from those who have experienced more of life than have I. Oftentimes helping craft a solution for a successful individual provides an opportunity for me to learn something that will allow me to help the next client more effectively. Part of the purpose of providing the case study format in part two is with the hope that some readers will be able to identify with one or more of the examples and perhaps even gain a different perspective on a problem they may have attempted to address unsuccessfully in the past.

As you read the book, remember that chapters one through eleven provide the most current and up-to-date information on estate tax reduction and wealth protection strategies. The case studies provide a practical application of the strategies. Hopefully, this works for you and your family. Enjoy.

Chapter 1

Why Everyone, Rich or Poor, or In-Between – Needs an Estate Plan

Estate tax reform–and possibly even estate tax repeal–is on the government's calendar. Does that mean you should place your estate planning on hold while you wait for word from Washington?

Absolutely not! While estate tax planning can be tremendously important for your heirs, paying attention to non-tax issues is vital for the success of any estate plan.

In truth, there's a lot more to estate planning than tax reduction. When clients come to our office, developing an estate plan might take three or four meetings–and we often don't even discuss estate taxes until the fourth one.

What sort of estate planning doesn't deal with estate taxes?

Making sure that your assets are passed to the desired recipients with a minimum of delay and family friction.

To avoid delay, you might want to take steps to see that your assets don't go through probate, which can be extremely costly, laborious, and time-consuming. Some types of assets, such as IRAs, annuities and insurance policies automatically pass to a named beneficiary without going through probate. The same is true of jointly owned property that will go to the surviving co-owner.

For other types of assets, it may be practical to hold them in trust: among the many advantages of trusts is the fact that assets they hold aren't subject to probate. Your wishes can be carried out immediately under the terms of the trust documents. (Later in this book you will learn about the comparative merits of revocable and irrevocable trusts but both types can keep your assets from going through probate.)

As far as family friction is concerned, the possibilities are literally endless. You might, for example, want to leave your estate evenly among your three children. But is it really "fair" to leave the successful corporate lawyer the same amount as you bequeath to the teacher and the military officer? If you want to divide your assets unevenly, how can hard feelings be avoided?

Often, the best approach is to leave some assets outright but to keep most of them in trust. The trustee, charged with managing trust assets, can make distributions to the trust beneficiaries, as needed. Moreover, assets held in trust are generally protected from lawsuits, creditors, divorcing spouses, etc.

Another problem may arise if your wealth is held largely in one asset, such as a family business or a real estate property. One of your heirs may make a fine manager but dividing the company or the property isn't practical. Here, one solution is to leave the prized asset to the one who's most capable while using life insurance to equalize the inheritances.

In yet another situation, suppose you're in a second marriage with most of your assets in an IRA. Naturally, you want to provide for your spouse but you also want to take care of your own children from your first marriage.

One possible technique to consider, in such situations, is the use of a qualified terminable interest property (QTIP) trust to inherit the IRA. Such a trust will distribute funds to your surviving spouse, for her lifetime, and then pass the trust assets to your children from your first marriage, after your surviving spouse's death.

On paper, this makes a great deal of sense. In the real world, though, your second spouse may not be that much older than the children from your first marriage. Assuming your surviving spouse lives to her normal life expectancy, there won't be much left in your IRA by the time she dies and your children can inherit.

Thus, if you were to adopt such a plan, you would be disinheriting your children. Is that acceptable? Perhaps, if your children are doing very well and you wanted to provide the maximum for your spouse. Chances are, though, that you won't want to disinherit your children.

With careful advanced planning, solutions can be developed. To begin with, you might name your spouse as the beneficiary of your IRA. At your death she'll inherit that account.

To even things out, you might buy insurance on your own life, naming your children as the beneficiaries. The amount of the insurance might be about the same as the amount in your IRA. Alternatively, the life insurance death benefit might be larger, anticipating future growth in the IRA.

For example, you might buy a 10-year term life insurance policy, payable to your children. Today, term life insurance is very competitive so the premiums likely will be relatively inexpensive, depending on your health. If you should die within the 10-year period, the insurance will provide an inheritance for your children while your wife can inherit your IRA.

What will happen after 10 years? This plan assumes your IRA will grow. At a 7% annual return, your IRA will practically double in 10 years. At that point, if the term insurance is too expensive to renew, you could divide your IRA in two, leaving one sizable account for your spouse and another sizable account to be divided among your children. Everyone will be provided for.

Such a strategy is not necessarily the estate plan that you should adopt, even in that situation. The message, rather, is that the real purpose of estate planning is to make sure that your assets are distributed to the people (and perhaps the charitable causes) that you intend to provide for. Ideally, such a distribution can take place as smoothly as possible, with no hard feelings among your survivors. Once those goals have been addressed, tactics may be pursued to reduce or eliminate estate taxes.

DIFFERENT STROKES

At different stages of your life, your estate plan will include different elements. A young couple with a small child, for example, might not have estate tax concerns but they will need to have a will.

In that will, they should name a guardian for their children, in case of a common disaster, and provide a financial allowance for the guardian. They probably will need life insurance, too. In the next chapter, I'll cover the basic building blocks that most estate plans should include.

Once you are established in your career, though, you may well have enough assets to be concerned about disability income provisions and estate tax. If so, what planning can you do, with the estate tax outlook so uncertain?

Some basic estate tax planning still makes sense. If you're married, you probably will want to leave a substantial portion, if not all, of your assets to your surviving spouse, who can inherit tax-free. That's the case under current law and probably will be the same after any legislative reform or repeal.

The crunch, though, may come at the death of your surviving spouse, when assets pass to the next generation. If you think a substantial amount of assets will be left, some planning will be necessary. Don't speculate on possible changes in the law: you need to plan for current law, and then make whatever changes might be necessary. The worst mistake is having no plan.

With no plan, your estate might wind up owing substantial amounts of tax, depending upon the date of death and the tax laws in effect at that time. With no plan, you can't take advantage of any tax-reduction strategies.

Of course, you might not think you'll need any tax reduction strategies because the so-called "death tax" will be repealed. In truth, it's doubtful that any such repeal will be enacted. Remember, estate taxes are paid by people with substantial estates and laws favoring the rich tend to be defeated by negative publicity.

In the coming years, the federal government will face enormous fiscal pressures from increased spending on Medicare and Social Security as well as larger national security outlays. In that climate it's hard to see how a law substantially reducing estate tax revenues can be passed. What's more, any repeal might well be followed in a future year with a reinstatement of the estate tax.

The bottom line is that you can't be certain you and your spouse will die in years when there is no estate tax. You can't even know how much of an estate tax exemption will be allowed. Therefore, you need to plan for a probable estate tax and the way to do so is to work with the law now in effect.

Under current (2004) law, estates over $1.5 million will be taxed. If you think your surviving spouse will leave a larger estate, it makes sense to leave money to your children, tax-free. A couple with $2 million in assets, for example, might arrange for $500,000 to pass to the children at the first death; assuming no asset growth in the interim, the survivor's estate also would escape estate tax. This plan can be changed if the tax laws change.

The problem with this solution, though, is that it leaves the surviving spouse with just $1.5 million instead of the $2 million in marital assets. The survivor may need the full $2 million for lifetime comfort and security.

These concerns may be addressed by leaving the entire $2 million to the surviving spouse. By the time the survivor dies, (1) more generous tax laws may be in force; (2) the survivor may have spent down the retirement fund so that the estate is not large enough to tax; or (3) some amount of estate tax may be due.

The bottom line is that it's a judgment call. Most likely, married couples with up to $2 million in total assets need not worry about the estate tax, as long as they can reasonably expect for one spouse to live another five years and they're at the point where they're drawing down their retirement funds.

That won't cover everyone, though. If your assets are over the $2 million mark, or you expect to accumulate that much in the future, some tax planning may be necessary. One approach, then, is to leave assets up to the current exemption amount ($1.5 million in 2004) to a trust; your spouse as well as your children can be the beneficiaries of the trust. Other assets can pass to your surviving spouse, free of estate tax. A well-crafted trust can provide the surviving spouse with access to the trust assets yet keep those assets from the taxable estate.

What if you expect your estate to be taxable mainly because of a large IRA? You might want to split the IRA into two accounts. One IRA can be left to your children, to take advantage of the estate tax exemption, while the other IRA passes to your surviving spouse. At your survivor's death, that IRA can pass to the children.

One common strategy is to use life insurance to provide the cash for estate tax payments so the IRA can remain intact for long-term tax deferral. You might consider buying convertible term insurance. If the laws are changed favorably, you can just drop the coverage, which is relatively inexpensive. On the other hand, if it turns out that you will need the insurance for estate taxes or for any other purpose, you can convert to a permanent life insurance policy that can be kept in force as long as it's needed.

For tax as well as non-tax estate planning, building in some flexibility can help you and your loved ones adapt to an ever-changing climate, increasing your chances for a happy ending.

Chapter 2
Estate Planning Basics

What should a thorough estate plan include? That depends on your circumstances, to a certain extent, but some elements are universal.

A WILL

If you've been putting off making a will because you're too busy, too young, or not rich enough–or merely because the thought of your own demise is too much to bear–you shouldn't delay any longer. Think of your family first, and prepare a will.

Without a will, you die "intestate." After your death a local court will appoint an administrator for your estate and your belongings will be distributed according to state law. Almost certainly, that disposition will not be exactly as you'd like.

In some states, half of all your assets may go to your children if you die without a will. Minor children may become wards of the state, with a court-appointed attorney who'll get paid off the top, before anything goes to your family. Your surviving spouse might have to account to a court for every penny spent on the children's behalf. Moreover, if your widowed spouse remarries, the new husband or wife may be entitled to the funds your spouse inherited from you, with no obligation to use them on behalf of your children. Other relatives of yours, including your parents, may have no claim on your estate.

If you have a will you can spell out the way you'd like your assets to be distributed and you can name an executor, who'll make sure your wishes are followed. When you draw up a will, you're in control.

Not only should your will be written, it should be drafted by an attorney. You and your spouse probably should have individual wills, rather than joint wills, for more flexibility.

After you've made your will, have copies made but sign only the original. Store the original in a safe place, such as a fireproof safe or a filing cabinet in your home or office. If you leave your will with your attorney, it may be misplaced.

Should you store the original in a bank safe-deposit box? Probably not. Many states seal those boxes immediately after death, to prevent tax cheating. There may be delays in getting the will. In any case, be sure your family knows where to find the original version of your will. I often suggest keeping a file with all of the "answers" in it. Information as to who to contact upon death, advisors, banks and brokerages can be listed; as should account and telephone numbers with contact information where possible. Bottom line is that dealing with a well-organized estate doesn't ease the grieving but it doesn't complicate it either.

If your will is held elsewhere, and the will names an executor, he or she can get a court's permission to open your safe deposit. Again, make sure that someone knows that you have a box, and where. You don't need to provide a key–a bank will drill open your box at a modest cost under a court order.

Although your will should be drafted by an experienced attorney, there are some traps you should know to avoid. For example, you should avoid bequests of specific assets because asset values can change dramatically. Instead of leaving stocks to one child and real estate to another child, you're probably better off leaving half the estate to each one.

Another approach is to leave each child, say, 40% of the estate with the remaining 20% going into a trust. This trust can be a "sprinkle" trust, where the trustee has discretion over distributions, so it becomes a safety net for any heir in need.

In general, you might want to limit outright bequests, especially if you've amassed a sizable estate. With outright bequests, if something should happen to you and your spouse, your children may come into millions of dollars, perhaps when they're very young.

Helen Parker, for example, is a widow whose husband had a $10 million net worth. He's dead so his will can't be changed, an irrevocable trust is in place, and she doesn't want to change her will because she's afraid of family antagonism. At her death, then, all of the money will go outright to their three children, two of whom are ne'er-do-wells while the third one doesn't need the money.

Fortunately, not everyone is locked in to a regretted estate plan. Alan and Susan Hawkins, who are both doctors, made up their wills 15 years ago, when they had no assets and a pile of school loans to pay off. Now they have about $6 million in net worth and a chance to double that, before they retire. They also have four young children, one with special needs. When they went over their old wills and discovered that each child would inherit in full, at age 21, they were dumbfounded.

The answer, for this couple, was to change their wills and leave most of their assets to a long-term trust. This is an "incentive trust," which includes provisions that will reward their children for reaching specific goals, such as getting a college education. At this couple's direction, the trust will pay distributions to their children if they work for certain types of community groups.

AN EXECUTOR

In your will you'll name an executor (sometimes known as an administrator or personal representative). After your death it will be up to your executor to inventory your assets, protect them against loss, pursue outstanding claims, pay bills, file tax returns, and pay taxes. Your executor will be responsible for protecting your heirs–and liable in case things go poorly.

Your spouse might not be a good choice for your executor. He or she probably will be too distraught after your death to act effectively. Often, grown children make the best executors. If that's not practical, you can name a professional advisor, such as an accountant or an attorney. Your estate will have to pay professionals for their services, so a fee schedule should be worked out in advance. (All executors are entitled to receive fees but family members may choose to waive them.)

Whomever you choose to serve as executor, get his or her consent to serve before naming someone in your will. You should make some provision for a backup executor, too, in case your original selection becomes unavailable, unwilling or unable to serve. Then, go over everything with your executor. Your executor should know what your assets are, how the title is held, and where the paperwork can be found. Your executor should see your will, or at least know what is in it, so there will be no surprises.

If your executor isn't a family member, he or she should meet your heirs, to get an idea of the personalities involved. Because your executor will be responsible for filing tax returns after your death, a meeting with your tax preparer likely will help things go more smoothly.

GUARDIANS

If you have minor children, you should name guardians in your will, in case both you and your spouse die in a common disaster. Again, you should get the guardians' permission before naming them.

Therefore, meetings and discussions with the potential candidates are essential before the final selection can be made. You can use these meetings to find out about an individual's or a married couple's willingness to become your children's guardian, their projected short- and long-range plans, and their viewpoints on issues that are crucial to you as parents. Do they share your values? Religious and political views: Will they provide supportive environment for your children?

LETTER OF INSTRUCTION

You probably won't change your will every time you buy a new car or sell some stock. Therefore, you may want to leave a letter of instruction, sometimes called a letter of intent, in addition to your will. In this letter you can spell out, in some detail, exactly what your assets are and how you'd like them distributed. Such a letter may help your executor locate assets and decide how to distribute them.

Suppose, for example, you have some valuable paintings you want to leave to your nephew or some jewelry you want a cousin to have. That type of bequest can be handled in a letter of instruction to the executor.

Although your bequests should be explained to everyone concerned while you're alive, there may be some things you'd rather not discuss during your lifetime. I am a proponent of full disclosure when and if heirs are able to handle the information. If someone receives more or less from the estate as a surprise, he/she is more likely to blame the other siblings. If things are explained up front, your heirs may not like it, but at least your intentions will be crystal clear. In that case, you might want to make a video recording, with a final message to your heirs as well as any instructions you care to provide. Even if you explain everything carefully to your heirs, it can't hurt to go over it all again, on tape and in writing, so everyone knows exactly what you had in mind.

If you use a word processor you can update the letter from time to time, printing out a current copy. Of course, family members or unrelated parties should know where this letter is kept. Preparing such a letter may be a good way to avoid family fights over your favorite things.

In some cases, this letter of instruction may be legally binding; some states permit changes without your having to re-write your will. Indeed, in some areas the practice is to refer to this letter as "Schedule A" of the will. However, in some states the instructions in this letter may not be legally binding so you need to work with an attorney who's knowledgeable about estate planning issues.

Other matters may be covered in this letter, from the identities of professional advisors to the location of key papers. In addition, you can use this letter to state your desires about funeral and burial arrangements, including the music you'd like to be played at your final service.

BENEFICIARIES

Despite all the above comments about the importance of having a will, the truth is that the disposition of many assets will not be covered by your will. Retirement plans, for example, pass to designated beneficiaries regardless of what's in your will. The same is true of life insurance proceeds and certain savings or investment accounts that are "payable on death" to specified beneficiaries. Assets held in trust are not subject to the provisions of your will, either.

Therefore, it's crucial to keep beneficiary designations up-to-date so that they reflect your current wishes. The IRA you set up 20 years ago may still carry an ex-spouse as the beneficiary, for example; changing the designation now may save your family a lot of grief in the future.

Indeed, for some people a will is likely to be a lengthy document, one they spend some time reading before giving final approval. These same people may handle the disposition of a six- or seven-figure IRA in less than a minute by jotting down a few words on a mass-produced form.

Many assets are subject to what might be called a complete financial succession plan. In a will or a trust, you can spell out what you'd like to happen, for example, if a beneficiary predeceases you, if a beneficiary is a minor or is incompetent, or if a married couple dies in a common disaster. However, there's no room for all of that on an IRA custodian's beneficiary designation form so many people don't provide for these circumstances.

Such carelessness may have huge costs for you and your loved ones. With proper planning, an IRA can span generations and pay out multiples of the amount you accumulate; in the absence of detailed instructions, though, tax deferral may be cut short. Even more important, the lack of a proper succession plan for your IRA may lead to familial strife and ease the way for future predators who are tempted by the substantial amounts involved.

How can you put your IRA on the right track and keep it there? One approach is to prepare a "retirement asset will" to supplement the custodian's or plan administrator's existing forms. This might allow you to select the choices and options otherwise available by law. For example, your retirement asset will can spell out your choices for IRA beneficiaries and contingent beneficiaries.

Such a document is essentially a customized beneficiary designation form. A custodian or plan administrator's own form is often too limiting. In many cases, for example, the IRA custodian's beneficiary designation is written in such a way that the surviving beneficiary will inherit the account, in case one beneficiary predeceases the owner. That may not be the desired result.

Suppose Dan Brown lists his two children, Mark and Marie, as IRA beneficiaries. Mark predeceases his father so the IRA account passes entirely to Marie while Mark's children (Dan's beloved grandchildren) get nothing. Because of such outcomes, if there is more than one IRA beneficiary you might want to consult a professional to make sure that your wishes are in agreement with the beneficiary designation form.

Drafting a customized beneficiary form to cover various contingencies is only the beginning, though. Such a form should be sent to the IRA custodian for acknowledgment and a signed copy should be returned to you. This form, in turn, should be kept in the same place as your will and other key documents. Beneficiary designations have been lost or not properly recorded. However, if you create a customized beneficiary form and keep it accessible, eventually it may be retrieved and used to instruct the custodian on the account's disposition.

Among some professionals, creating and preserving such documents has become routine. Even with such a form, though, you and your professional advisors need to follow up, during your lifetime and afterwards, to make sure the custodians comply.

Unfortunately, not every custodian will accept a customized beneficiary form or agree to all of its terms. When an IRA custodian (which might be a bank, brokerage firm, insurer, or mutual fund company) acknowledges one of these forms, it may be acknowledging receipt of the form rather than acknowledging an agreement to comply with its terms. In some cases, you may have to sign a document relieving the plan administrator or IRA custodian of liability for accepting a customized form.

Custodians dislike the uncertainties such forms may create. Suppose your plan calls for some portion of your IRA to be left to a child, to use up the amount that's exempt from estate tax, while the balance goes to your spouse. There's no way of knowing how much will be needed to use up the estate tax exemption, at some point in the future, or even if there will be an estate tax.

If you have a reluctant custodian, you might name a trust as IRA beneficiary. Then the disposition instructions can be included in the trust documents, which can be as detailed as any will. If an IRA is left to a trust it's the trustee, not the custodian, that's responsible for making the decisions.

Whether your plan calls for a customized beneficiary form or a trust to be named as IRA beneficiary, the document should be coordinated with your will. Changes need to be made in case of events such as a beneficiary's death or the account owner's divorce. Otherwise, an IRA inadvertently might be left to a former spouse.

Keep in mind that a detailed IRA beneficiary form is really a "wish list." There's no guarantee that your beneficiary will carry out your wishes. Nevertheless, having a customized beneficiary form can spell out your plan and make it possible for your beneficiary to follow through.

Moreover, IRS regulations on IRA distributions make a detailed beneficiary designation extremely important. Under these rules, a designated beneficiary will not be determined until September 30th of the year following the death of the IRA owner.

How can you designate a beneficiary a year or two after your death? Not via sèances or Ouija boards. The regulations underscore the importance of naming a beneficiary and a contingent beneficiary. The primary beneficiary can disclaim his interest up until September 30th of the following year. Then the contingent beneficiary would become the designated beneficiary, able to use his life expectancy for required withdrawals. Such a plan might lead to many decades of tax deferral, but only if the right paperwork is in place. When everything is spelled out, your IRA can stand for an Intensely-Reasoned Aftermath.

FUNERAL AND BURIAL ARRANGEMENTS

Does it make sense to pay for your funeral in advance? The main advantage of prepaying for funeral and burial arrangements is peace of mind. Your survivors won't have to make those arrangements during a time of stress. That's especially true if your loved ones live far away from you and travel delays might complicate matters.

Most funeral homes offer these plans. Ask your friends and acquaintances for the names of reputable funeral homes, and then request their brochures. Buy the service you really want–don't let yourself get pressured into paying for unnecessary rituals.

Consult with your attorney before making any commitment and be sure to describe any arrangements you make in the letter of instruction that accompanies your will. Otherwise, your executor may pay again for funeral arrangements or a burial plot, unaware that you've already prepaid them.

Make sure your executor has all the details and any deeds or contracts are in an accessible place. Don't put your funeral and burial wishes in your will if the will is kept in a safe-deposit box. That box may not be opened until after the funeral—too late for burial instructions.

Technically, funeral arrangements are the responsibility of family members rather than your executor. However, there may be some confusion as to which family members should make the decisions. Because the executor eventually will pay the bills (out of your estate), it's probably better to entrust that person with the necessary documents.

WORST-CASE SCENARIOS

The estate plan elements described above will take effect at the time of your death. In many cases, though, death may come after a period of incapacity. If so, a large portion of your estate may be lost to various caregivers, caretakers, and just plain takers. Thus, a comprehensive estate plan will include preparations for possible incapacity. You want to be sure someone you trust will be making financial decisions and possibly shift the financial burden to an insurance company.

One seemingly simple way to prepare for incapacity is to move your assets into joint name with a son or daughter. Then your child can sell stocks from the jointly held brokerage account or jointly held stock certificates, if you're not able. The downside? Joint ownership overrides whatever is in your will. If your brokerage account is in joint name, all of those assets go to your co-owner at your death. Your other would-be heirs will be shut out.

A better way is to move assets into a trust. A trustee can sell the shares, if needed to pay your living expenses, yet the trust documents can provide for any disposition that's desired, after your death.

If the amounts involved are small, though, you may not want to incur the expense of creating a trust (expect to spend a few thousand dollars on legal fees) or go through the trouble of re-titling assets to a trust. An alternative, in these circumstances, is to execute a power of attorney, authorizing someone to act on your behalf (see below).

What if you've done none of the above and you become incompetent? Your family's only option may be to petition a court, asking for someone to be named your guardian. Such a process can take time and stir up hard feelings among family members. Your entire family will be better off with some advanced planning.

POWER OF ATTORNEY

As mentioned, you might lose command of your mental capabilities as you grow older. If this happens, a series of poor financial decisions could wipe out your estate, leaving nothing for your heirs.

To prevent such a catastrophe, you should create a power of attorney, a document that enables someone else to act on your behalf. Naturally, you must have absolute confidence in the person you name.

You might execute a durable power of attorney, one that takes effect immediately and will remain in effect if you become incompetent. Another option is to create a springing power of attorney, which will not become effective until one or more doctors attest that you have lost the ability to handle your own affairs.

Some attorneys prefer durable powers because they're more convenient. However, you may not be comfortable knowing that someone can use a power of attorney at any time, to take over your assets, so you might choose the springing power. Generally, putting a springing power into effect is not difficult, when required by an individual's circumstances.

If your state doesn't recognize springing powers, you may be able to achieve the same result with a durable power accompanied by a letter stating that this power will go into effect if certain events take place; your attorney can hold both documents until they're needed.

You can't be careless about your power of attorney. Not only must it be durable, it should contain specific authorization for your agent to perform the activities you desire.

A run-of-the-mill power of attorney (the short form you can pick up for a few dollars at a stationery store) is non-durable, meaning that it will no longer be effective if you (the person granting the power, known as the principal) lose your capacity to make decisions.

On the other hand, a durable power of attorney remains in effect even if you become incapacitated. The person you name (your agent) can file tax returns, make gifts, disclaim property, and make retirement plan distribution decisions, etc., on your behalf.

Even with a durable power of attorney, though, things can go awry. First of all, you have to name someone you absolutely trust, as your agent. You may want to name two co-agents, stating that they must act together.

You also should hire a knowledgeable lawyer to draw up your document. An oversight can be extremely costly.

In one case, an elderly woman appointed her nephew as her agent on a durable power of attorney when she was extremely ill (she died two months later). The nephew, wishing to reduce estate taxes, made 38 gifts of $10,000 apiece to various friends and relatives. Under the law in effect then, those gifts could be covered by annual estate tax exclusion, and removed from the aunt's estate, tax-free. (The limit is now $11,000 per recipient per year.)

The IRS attempted to restore this $380,000 to the aunt's estate, and the issue wound up in court. The nephew testified that he had discussed the idea of making gifts, in order to reduce estate taxes, with his aunt. According to the nephew he drew up a list of 40 possible recipients, read the names to his aunt, and received 38 nods of approval from his weakening aunt.

This testimony did not convince the court. These events took place in California, where powers of attorney must specifically state that the agent has the authority to make gifts on the principal's behalf. (Many states have similar laws.) Here, the power of attorney did not include this authorization so the gifted assets were effectively returned to the aunt's taxable estate, at a cost of over $140,000 in estate tax.

Therefore, if you choose to include a power of attorney in your estate plan, make sure that it spells out the agent's ability to make gifts to family members or to non-relatives, and that other planning tactics also are mentioned.

Some financial institutions require the use of their own power of attorney forms. As a result, you should check with your banks, brokers, etc., after a power of attorney has been drawn up. Send a copy to each institution, asking if there's any problem with the form. Make sure the power allows the holder to continue to do things consistent with the estate plan, like make gifts. The omission of this could be disastrous, especially if ongoing gifts were necessary for obligations to charitable beneficiaries or to pay life insurance premiums on a trust owned policy.

After you execute a power of attorney, you should update it every year or two, which will increase the likelihood your power will be honored. Otherwise, a challenger with an adverse interest may claim that it's invalid. Each time it's renewed, have several original powers of attorney executed and notarized, because some institutions will insist upon keeping one of these powers in their files.

REVOCABLE TRUSTS

Commonly known as living trusts, revocable trusts are created while you are alive and can be changed, if desired. Once assets have been transferred into a living trust, they avoid the time and expense of probate, at the trust creator's death.

Perhaps more important, a living trust is a valuable tool for incapacity planning. As you grow older, you may not be able to manage your own affairs. Without a plan in place, your relatives might have to go to court in an effort to get a guardian named. If more than one person desires to be the guardian, a nasty public dispute may arise.

Such problems can be avoided if you have transferred your assets into a living trust. Typically, you will be the trustee, in control of the trust assets. You'll also name a co-trustee or successor trustee, if you become incompetent, that the other party can take over for seamless continuity in managing the trust assets, with no need to petition a court.

(Remember, the benefits of a living trust will be attained only if you take the time to actually transfer assets into the trust.)

Not all trusts are revocable, of course. As you'll see in Chapter 5, you also can create irrevocable trusts, during your lifetime or at your death. Indeed, revocable trusts eventually can become irrevocable, at your death. Irrevocable trusts are generally used for tax planning rather than for incapacity planning because assets moved to an irrevocable trust are out of your control and thus out of your taxable estate.

LONG-TERM CARE INSURANCE

In addition to a power of attorney and a revocable trust, long-term care (LTC) insurance may be necessary for incapacity planning. Such policies pay benefits to insured individuals who no longer can care for themselves. If family members are not willing or able, third parties must provide the needed care, either at home or in an institution.

Remember, the concept of "estate planning" assumes that you have an estate to plan for. However, as you get older you might grow frail, dependent upon others for constant care. If you need to go into an institution or hire professional home care aides, the cost may be enormous, wiping out your life's savings.

The average cost of staying in a nursing home in the U.S. now tops $50,000 per year, and those outlays can top $100,000 a year in some areas. At those rates, years of custodial care might cost hundreds of thousands of dollars. This may be an enormous burden, especially for a married couple if one spouse must maintain a residence while the other requires care in a nursing home.

Even if long-term care can be provided at home, the amounts paid to qualified people may be immense. Moreover, your aging parent or parents may need years of expensive care, effectively moving money you might have inherited into the pockets of a nursing home operator. To prevent such an occurrence, you (and perhaps your siblings) might want to help provide long-term care (LTC) insurance for your parents.

For yourself and your spouse as well as your parents, LTC insurance may be desirable. A policy that pays, say, $200 per day would contribute nearly $75,000 per year towards the cost of needed care.

Most people do not need long-term care until they are quite elderly. At that age, though, LTC insurance may be extremely expensive. According to the American Health Care Association, someone who buys LTC insurance at age 65 would pay about twice as much per year as would be paid for a similar policy, bought at age 55. Someone who waits until age 79 would pay around four times as much per year as a 65-year-old would pay.

Moreover, people who wait to buy this coverage may incur certain health conditions that will prevent them for acquiring LTC insurance at all. The younger and healthier you are when purchasing LTC insurance, the lower the cost will be. Consequently, you might want to look into acquiring LTC insurance while you're in your 50s or 60s and still relatively healthy.

LTC insurance can be extremely complicated. It is important to buy an adequate amount of coverage but not to overpay for excess benefits; it is vital to acquire a policy that will pay for at-home as well as nursing-home care if certain activities of daily living (ADLs) cannot be performed. In addition, LTC insurance companies frequently offer a variety of features that may or may not be worth paying for.

WHAT SHOULD YOU CONSIDER WHEN SHOPPING FOR LTC INSURANCE?

Insurance company quality. Generally, you should buy LTC insurance from an established company in excellent financial condition. Leading name-brand companies are likely to maintain premiums. Major insurers don't want to attract negative attention in the media and they don't want to trigger adverse legislation. Therefore, they can't afford to be too aggressive raising rates so it's more likely your initial premium will remain fixed.

In addition, such companies are more careful about the people they insure and they have ample financial resources, so you can expect them to be around in the future, if you claim benefits under their policies.

Before buying LTC insurance, find out whether the company has raised rates for existing policyholders. Some companies have made honest mistakes and priced their policies too low: claims have been higher than expected, so they've had to raise premiums.

Other companies have used bait-and-switch tactics, enticing consumers with prices they knew would be raised in the future. Either way, you should avoid the companies that have increased premiums in the past.

Inflation protection. Your policy should have an increasing benefit. If you buy a policy that pays $100 per day, by the time you need care, which might be 10 years from now or longer, that $100 won't go very far. A good policy will increase that benefit each year, so it might pay $150 or $200 per day when you need care.

Full coverage. Home care is now as expensive as care in an institution so your LTC policy should pay benefits in either situation. There is an exception to this rule, though. Single women–especially widows–who live alone probably are better off in a facility if they need care.

Widows may be better off in a nursing home or assisted living facility, if they need care, so they might as well buy an LTC insurance policy that covers only facility care. Such policies might be 40% less expensive than policies covering home health care as well. Often, elderly people buy unnecessary home care coverage because they think this coverage will keep them out of a nursing home. The truth, though, is that your health will determine where you're cared for.

Tax angles. Another wrinkle that should be addressed before buying LTC insurance: taxes. Federal law permits deductions for the premiums, in some cases, but only 4% of all taxpayers will qualify. Therefore, most states offer tax breaks of their own; often, you can take state income tax deductions for the premiums not deductible on your federal tax return.

Business owners may be able to benefit from another LTC insurance tax break. If your company is set up as a regular C corporation, the corporation can provide LTC insurance for yourself and for your spouse, too. The premiums will be deductible. What's more, you don't have to provide this coverage for your other employees.

Combination plans. Your disability insurance policy or your life insurance policy may provide some LTC protection. Increasingly, life insurers are offering LTC riders. With such a rider, if long-term care is needed, a portion of the death benefit can be paid out each month. Moreover, a few companies offer LTC coverage as an extra feature with their variable annuities. In addition, some disability policies will automatically become LTC policies at a certain point, perhaps after retirement.

The bottom line is that America is growing older and the need for long-term care is on the increase. There is scant chance of government funding, except for the impoverished, so it's up to you to make your own arrangements. All manner of insurance companies are offering LTC coverage, in many different forms, so the earlier you start to do your homework the better your chances of passing this intimidating final exam.

FINAL THOUGHTS

Other documents, such as a living will and a health care proxy, may be part of your estate plan. In addition, you probably will want to keep a list of all your important documents, along with their location, to make life easier for your executor.

However, there's more to a solid estate plan than a pile of paperwork. For a truly successful wealth transfer plan you should sit down with your loved ones and explain how you've handled your assets, which advisors have been providing assistance, and what steps your heirs should take after they inherit.

TITLE GAMES

Another vital aspect of your estate plan is deciding how your property should be owned. Holding property in joint name has advantages but there may be traps, too. Suppose your mother, age 85, has $100,000 worth of securities that cost her $20,000. If she dies and leaves her portfolio to you, you'll inherit with a "step-up in basis." You can sell the inherited securities and owe no capital gains tax on all the appreciation during your mother's lifetime.

But what if your mother names you as joint owner during her lifetime, so that you can handle those securities for her? Will you get a basis step-up on your mother's $50,000 but no step-up on your $50,000 share?

Fortunately, the full tax break need not be lost. If two co-owners are not married to each other, the estate of the first owner to die will include a share of the property based on the portion of the original purchase price furnished by the decedent. Thus, if your mother owns securities outright and adds you as a joint owner, 100% of the securities will be included in her estate. You'll get a full step-up in basis after you inherit.

On the downside, if your mother names you as joint owner, no one else can inherit those assets, even your other siblings. If your sister who lives around the corner from your mother is the one whose name goes on the brokerage account, then all of the securities will go to your sister and none to you.

In these circumstances, a trust may work best to protect all parties. You or one of your siblings could be a co-trustee, empowered to act if your mother became incapacitated.

Similarly, if you hold jointly-owned property it will always pass to your surviving co-owner, no matter what you put in your will. If you change your brokerage account into joint name with your son Bob, at your death all of the securities in that account will go to Bob while your daughters Carla and Constance will be shut out. So you should consider changing from joint ownership arrangements, if that's not your intent, and be careful about adding one relative's name to your home, bank accounts, or investments.

Moreover, your situation will be different if you live in one of several states (including California and Texas) where community property laws apply. In essence, all property acquired by either spouse during a marriage as a result of the labors of either spouse is considered to be community property. Regardless of how such property might be titled, it belongs to a marital partnership between two 50-50 owners. Upon death, each spouse can control the disposition of his or her one-half community property interest. Thus, you only own half of community property, for purposes of deciding how to distribute such property at your death.

COVER YOUR ASSETS

An estate plan also should be an asset protection plan. After all, you won't have much to leave to your loved ones if your assets are wiped out in a frivolous lawsuit. How can you keep creditors away from your personal assets?

Contribute the maximum amount permitted to an employer-sponsored retirement plan. This not only will defer taxes, it will protect those assets. The Employee Retirement Income Security Act (ERISA), covers "Qualified" retirement plans, which is a federal law. Your creditors can't attach money you build up in 401(k)s, etc. The only party with access to these plans is the IRS, in case you owe taxes.

However, not all retirement plans are covered by ERISA. IRAs, Roth IRAs, SIMPLE IRAs, and simplified employee pensions (SEPs) are all not ERISA plans so they are not creditor-protected by ERISA. Nevertheless, these retirement funds enjoy some protection from creditors through barriers established by state law, which differ greatly from state to state. Again, if you owe federal tax, money that you hold in an IRA, SEP, etc., can be attached.

Recent changes in pension law may help lawsuit-plagued business owners. If you run your business as a corporation and have employee participants, it may pay to investigate whether establishing a 401(k) plan and rolling over IRA funds to this plan makes sense. IRA funds may now be freely transferred to 401(k)s and the funds rolled over may be protected under ERISA.

Self-employed individuals should also investigate establishing a Keogh plan for themselves and rolling over IRA assets to the plan. In some states, Keogh plans enjoy full protection, providing contributions were made while the debtor was solvent and an income tax deduction was allowed.

Make partners out of your family members. You can shelter securities held in brokerage accounts or owned directly by placing them inside a Family Limited Partnership (FLP). Someone who sues you and receives an award for damages may not be able to collect from the FLP's assets.

Instead of an FLP, you might want to create a Limited Liability Company (LLC) to hold the family's securities. An LLC offers more asset protection. With an FLP, the general partner generally has unlimited liability if sued. If you hold a general partnership unit as well as other assets, those assets may be vulnerable to creditors.

Some techniques may be used to reduce the general partner's liability: a corporation or an LLC might be formed to act as the general partner of an FLP. The LLC is a simpler arrangement because you can avoid the extra steps an FLP may involve.

LLCs offer asset protection to all members. You can even have a one-person LLC to isolate a particular asset. Someone who owns apartment buildings, for example, might use a separate LLC for each one. If something goes wrong with one property, the problem won't spill over to the others.

Transfer property into an irrevocable trust. Once you shift assets into an irrevocable trust, it's difficult to regain use of those assets. However, your family may continue to enjoy use of the assets, depending on your choices of trustee and beneficiaries.

Some irrevocable trusts may be set up with terms that go on for decades, providing asset protection for your children and grandchildren, too. These trusts may keep assets in the family in case of a divorce, years in the future.

Alaska has ratified trust rules that protect assets from creditors while still providing trust creators with some access to the trust funds. In essence, some of the trust assets must be held in an Alaska institution, with at least one Alaska trustee. Delaware trusts also may be helpful.

Unfortunately, transferring assets to a trust after you've been sued, or when a suit is anticipated, is unlikely to protect those assets. Transferring assets "after the fact" to a trust would still subject these transfers to federal fraudulent transfer statutes. Assuming a claim has already been filed, any transfers made may be deemed an attempt to delay, hinder or defeat creditors and incur the wrath of the courts. The transfer might be disregarded and the assets exposed to creditors.

Go offshore. If you wish to be extremely aggressive about creditor protection, offshore jurisdictions may provide greater creditor protection than U.S. domiciled trusts. Some offshore jurisdictions have trust laws that discourage creditors' claims. Offshore trusts can be more costly to establish and maintain, however.

Despite the costs, offshore asset protection trusts are increasingly popular. Insurance hikes have forced people to do without coverage or with less coverage than they'd like. That goes for malpractice insurance as well as general liability insurance.

Unable to attain full protection with liability insurance, some people are turning to offshore trusts. They establish trusts in jurisdictions such as the Cook Islands, Isle of Man, and Nevis, where creditors may find it difficult to proceed against our clients' assets. Some offshore trusts have run into problems in the U.S. courts but a well-crafted trust should hold up, so make sure you work with an experienced attorney.

Have your company own your car. To protect a vehicle from creditors, you might lease a new one each year with zero down so that little or no equity builds up. A creditor can only take what actually belongs to you, not what the bank owns. Moreover, if you run your business and the vehicle is used for a legitimate business purpose, the corporation should own the vehicle. Such ownership may keep a car from being attached by creditors.

Alternatively, your spouse could own the family cars. As long as you're in a sound marriage, this is a simple way to keep assets from the reach of your creditors.

Insure your portfolio. In some states, life insurance policies and annuity contracts are beyond the reach of creditors. If you live in such a state, you might want to do your investing inside a protected variable annuity or variable life insurance policy. Either way, you can direct your investment among several types of professionally managed sub-accounts.

Be businesslike. George Franklin is an entrepreneur whose business went under. Subsequently, a vendor tried to collect on an invoice. When the company could not pay, the vendor went after George's personal assets.

George claimed that the debts were not his but were those of the corporation. However, the judge ruled for the vendor. The invoices were in George's name, not a company name. The original paperwork had his name but did not refer to his title as company president. The business name listed did not have the proper "Inc." behind the name because George was rushing and failed to properly set up the vendor account.

Hopefully, your company will be able to pay off all its vendors but you never know what the future will bring so it pays to take steps to protect your personal assets from creditors. When establishing your enterprise, consult with a business or corporate attorney and a CPA. Your personal assets are subject to creditor's claims if you are a sole proprietorship or general partner in a partnership. If you use a structure such as an a LLC, S or C corporation you can limit the amount of exposure of your personal assets to creditors if you take certain steps:

- Document that you have properly maintained separate books and records for your business.
- Manage the business properly by filing forms such as annual reports on time.
- Make no attempts to fraudulently convey assets from the business to you or to your personal representatives, in order to avoid possible judgments or seizures.
- Bottom line; respect the entity.

BREATHE LIFE (INSURANCE) INTO YOUR ESTATE PLAN

If you have dependents, you should have coverage to replace your lost income, in case of your untimely death. When someone who is producing income dies, the survivors are likely to miss that source of cash flow. Life insurance proceeds can fill the financial gap.

Therefore, it is vital that income producers with dependents carry ample amounts of life insurance. On the other hand, paying for unnecessary insurance probably will not be desirable. The challenge, for most people, is to purchase the amount of life insurance that is genuinely needed.

Some insurers buyers and sellers use "six times income" as a rule of thumb. For example, an individual earning $250,000 per year would be advised to buy $1.5 million worth of insurance coverage. Such generalities, though, fail to account for individual circumstances.

A more sophisticated approach takes more time but is more likely to result in an accurate outcome. To begin, you should forecast how much your survivors would need to maintain a comfortable lifestyle. You might start by determining how much your family now spends each year: gross income minus taxes and savings. (For consistency, keep all calculations on an after-tax basis.)

After estimating how much your survivors would need, future income might be projected. Your surviving spouse might continue to work; income might come from rental property. In many cases, Social Security benefits will be available.

Suppose, for example, Robert Evans estimates that his surviving family members will need $100,000 per year to maintain their way of life in case of his untimely death. Income from all sources is forecast at $40,000 per year, leaving a $60,000 annual shortfall.

Robert assumes that an investment portfolio, if handled prudently, could generate a 5% annual return, after-tax. Therefore, a $1.2 million portfolio would be able to provide his family with $60,000 per year for living expenses. Adding in extraordinary expenses, such as college costs, Robert decides he would like his survivors to have $1.5 million in investable assets.

At present, Robert's investment portfolio is $500,000. (That excludes the amount in his tax-deferred retirement plan, which he wants to preserve.) Therefore, he concludes he needs $1 million worth of life insurance coverage.

Projected survivors' annual expenses	$	100,000
Projected survivors' annual income	$	(40,000)
Projected annual shortfall needed from portfolio	$	60,000
Desired portfolio, assuming 5% after-tax return	$	1,200,000
Additional future expenses (e.g., college bills)	$	300,000
Total amount of desired portfolio for survivors	$	1,500,000
Size of current portfolio	$	(500,000)
Amount of life insurance necessary	$	1,000,000

Once a desired amount of insurance coverage has been determined, the type of policy must be selected. Life insurance policies fall into two major categories:

Term insurance. The insured individual is covered for a specific time period. Premium payments increase if continued coverage is desired. To keep future costs under control, you may buy "level-premium term," which offers fixed premiums for perhaps 10, 15, or 20 years.

Permanent insurance. Insurance coverage is meant to last indefinitely, at a set premium payment. Permanent insurance includes an investment account commonly known as the "cash value." Excess premiums go into this account. As the insured individual grows older, and term insurance costs would become prohibitive, the cash value may be tapped for the required premiums, keeping the policy in force.

Generally, you're better off buying inexpensive term insurance. Why pay $5,000 or $10,000 per year for a permanent life insurance policy when you can get the same amount of term insurance for $1,000 per year?

There are circumstances, though, when permanent insurance makes sense. First, you have to be able to afford the extra premiums without cutting into your lifestyle. If you were going to invest those extra thousands of dollars anyway, or if you need the discipline to help you invest rather than spend, permanent insurance may be a good investment vehicle.

Second, this has to be a truly long-term commitment. If you're only going to need insurance for 10 years or so, buy term. But if you see your need for life insurance stretching for 20, 30 years or longer, a permanent policy might pay off.

Tax advantages may make permanent insurance the better choice, in selected circumstances. For all insurance policies (term and permanent), death benefits generally escape income tax. Permanent policies get two more tax breaks.

For one, any cash value buildup won't be taxed. You might pay $200,000 worth of premiums, over 20 years, and see your cash value grow to $400,000 or $500,000 or even more. No taxes will be due on that growth.

For another, you can tap the cash value, tax-free, via loans and withdrawals. In effect, you can put tax-free investment income into your pocket.

The catch? You can't take out too much from the cash value so you have to tread carefully, probably with the help of a knowledgeable advisor. You might, for example, be able to pull out $40,000 or $50,000 a year from a $500,000 cash value but if you take out more, the policy will lapse and all the taxes will be due.

This strategy isn't for everyone. You won't be able to draw down all the cash value: you must keep enough in there to keep the policy alive and ultimately pay out to your beneficiary. Nevertheless, if you have a truly long-term game plan, the tax advantages may make permanent life insurance the way to protect those you hold dear.

PLANNING POINT – LEAVE $$ FOR SPOUSE AND CHILDREN IN A WEALTH TRUST

If you think you won't need to tap the cash value, you might hold a life insurance policy in an irrevocable trust, such as The Wealth

Trust® that will be described later. Inside a trust, the insurance benefits won't be subject to estate tax.

In some cases, the insurance proceeds can be used to pay estate taxes so your other assets will remain intact. If the proceeds aren't needed for estate tax they can remain inside the trust. In effect, the trust becomes a "family bank" for your surviving spouse and children. If the proceeds aren't needed, wealth can build within the trust; if a need arises, distributions can be made to your loved ones. Inside the trust, moreover, the insurance proceeds will be protected from squandering, creditors, and estate tax.

THERE ARE SEVERAL FORMS OF PERMANENT INSURANCE

With whole-life or universal life insurance, the cash value is meant to increase steadily. Returns often are comparable to the yields on investment-grade corporate bonds. In recent years, universal life has gained popularity because these policies may allow some flexibility in the amount of premiums that must be paid. These policies are becoming more and more flexible with current assumption pricing and the availability of secondary guarantees to take some of the uncertainty out of contracts.

With variable life insurance, policyholders direct their premiums among several investment sub-accounts, which usually include equity funds. Therefore, you may have both the increased risk and the potential for higher rewards presented by the stock market. Variable Universal Life (VUL) policies appeal to some buyers because they offer both flexibility and the possibility of outstanding buildup, within the cash value.

Even if your need for family protection diminishes with time, life insurance may still serve valuable estate planning purposes:

- Estate liquidity. Life insurance proceeds might be used to pay an estate tax bill and additional final expenses (such as funeral costs) so that your other assets remain intact.

However, those proceeds themselves may be subject to estate tax if a non-spouse is the beneficiary.

To avoid estate tax, an insurance policy may be transferred to a trust. After three years, life insurance proceeds can be excluded from the insured individual's taxable estate. (Such a transfer may create gift tax consequences so a knowledgeable tax advisor should be consulted.) Alternatively, a newly issued policy may be purchased by a trust.

- Extended tax-deferral. If life insurance can be used to satisfy an estate tax obligation, your IRA or other tax-deferred retirement plan need not be depleted. The more money left in the plan, the greater the amounts that can be paid out to the plan beneficiaries, over their remaining life expectancy.
- Business succession. For many business owners, an interest in a closely held company makes up a substantial portion of net worth. If you're in that situation, ensuring that your heirs receive fair value for that interest can be a challenge.

  Again, life insurance can provide the needed funds. In one common scenario, the proceeds from a policy on your life will be payable to your successor or to your surviving co-owner. Then those proceeds can be used to buy your interest from your heirs, at a previously agreed-upon price or valuation method.

  Another application might involve so-called "key executive" coverage. In case you die while playing an active role in your company, life insurance proceeds might help the business obtain a replacement and maintain the company's value.
- Estate equalization. Life insurance proceeds may help resolve awkward estate planning dilemmas. For example, suppose that Nancy Gordon has a $10 million estate, including a wholly owned company valued at $5 million. She wishes to leave the company to her son Keith but that would mean smaller bequests for her other two children, Laurel and Melissa.

A $5 million life insurance policy can help Nancy be fair to all of her children. If Laurel and Melissa were the co-beneficiaries, each would receive $2.5 million as well as $2.5 million apiece from estate assets. Therefore, they would receive the same amount of assets as Keith, who inherits the $5 million company.

- Roth IRA Conversions. As mentioned, estate planning often calls for the current purchase of life insurance to meet an anticipated estate tax obligation. The insurance proceeds can be used so that estate assets needn't be liquidated.

  However, recent legislation leads many people to anticipate no estate tax obligation. If the estate tax exemption goes up to $3.5 million (or even $2 million) and stays there, many estates will go untaxed. When using life insurance it should provide a competitive internal rate of return (IRR) defined as dollars in versus death benefit out to heirs. If there are no estate taxes the investment for your heirs is still a good one.

  Nevertheless, life insurance may prove valuable to help your heirs meet an income tax obligation. For example, the insurance proceeds may make a Roth IRA conversion feasible.

  Suppose you build up a $1 million IRA and you'd like to convert it to a Roth IRA, so that all future withdrawals are tax-free, but such a conversion would trigger $1 million in taxable income and cost about $400,000 in income tax. You don't have that much cash and it doesn't seem wise to deplete the converted IRA.

  In this scenario, you die and leave the $1 million IRA to your spouse. She can roll that IRA into her own account and name new beneficiaries.

  Good planning might call for you to include a life insurance policy in an irrevocable trust, such as The Wealth Trust® (see page 97), payable after your death. If this is the case, your surviving spouse could convert the IRA she now owns to a

Roth IRA and The Wealth Trust® could lend her the money to pay the $400,000 income tax bill.

Now that your spouse holds a Roth IRA, rather than a traditional IRA, no distributions are required. That Roth IRA might grow to $1.5 million or $2 million, at the time of her death. Then her beneficiaries (probably your children or grandchildren) could take out many millions of dollars over their life expectancies–and never pay one penny of income tax.

Good planning is necessary to achieve such a desirable result. A Roth IRA conversion is allowed only if the IRA owner's income is $100,000 ($150,000 if married) for the year.

Therefore, steps should be taken to see that the surviving spouse's income is under that ceiling in the year of the conversion. They can have any amount of income the year before or the year after, without affecting the Roth IRA conversion.

THE DEATH (AND REBIRTH?) OF ESTATE TAX

Although estate planning needn't focus on taxes, you shouldn't ignore estate taxes altogether. Unfortunately, current law doesn't make things easy.

As things now stand, everyone can leave up to $1.5 million worth of assets, free of estate tax. That number is expected to increase in steps to $3.5 million, for people who die in 2009.

People who die in 2010 can leave any amount because the estate tax is scheduled to disappear. (There may be some income tax on appreciated assets, though.) Then, beginning in 2011, the estate tax is supposed to reappear, with a $1.5 million exemption.

How can you plan for this here today, gone-tomorrow, back-the-day-after-tomorrow scenario? Your best option is to plan for the worst: anticipate death occurring in 2004, when the exemption will be $1.5 million.

Now, $1.5 million may seem like a great deal but that doesn't mean $1.5 million of cash in the bank.

At your death, your executor will add up all of your assets: investments, real estate, collectibles, retirement plans, etc. Exemptions are allowed for bequests to your spouse and to charity; for all other bequests, amounts in excess of $1 million are taxed at 41% or higher.

Say you leave a $1 million IRA, a $500,000 house, and a $1 million investment portfolio to your daughter. Your estate will total $2.5 million and over $400,000 in federal estate tax will be due.

To complicate matters, there is no knowing when you will die, how large an estate you'll leave, whether your heirs will need an inheritance, or what the tax laws will be at the time.

The best solution, then, may be the build a great deal of flexibility into your estate plan. In the above example, you might leave all of your assets to your daughter but you also can identify other heirs in case your daughter disclaims (waives) some or all of those assets.

Let's see how this might play out. You live for another 40 years, gradually spending down your $2.5 million in assets. At the time of your death, you leave $800,000 to your daughter, an amount too small to be affected by estate taxes. Your daughter accepts this inheritance and no problems arise.

On the other hand, say you die with most of your $2.5 million estate intact. You daughter, in the meantime, has prospered in her own career and in her investments so she has considerable wealth on her own. If she accepts your inheritance, she'll be receiving money she doesn't need. If she invests that money and it continues to grow, she may be creating or expanding the estate tax payable at her death. In this situation, she can disclaim her right to her inheritance.

If the idea of this flexibility seems appealing to you, how should you set up your estate plan? You might provide that any disclaimed assets will go to your daughter's two children, your grandchildren. Assuming they are capable young adults, this might be an acceptable plan. It's true that there is a generation-skipping transfer (GST) tax on bequests to grandchildren, but you can leave up to $1.1 million worth of assets, exempt from the GST.

In reality, though, your situation might not be so clear-cut. Your grandchildren might be minors, or they might be adults who are vulnerable to predators, bad marriages, and so on. In essence, you may be reluctant to see them receive large amounts of money outright. Moreover, when the time comes to disclaim assets, your daughter might be reluctant to give them away, for fear she'll need them some day.

Often, the best solution is for you to create a trust such as The Wealth Trust®, with your daughter as well as your grandchildren (and perhaps other loved ones) as trust beneficiaries. Then the trustee can distribute assets to your daughter, if necessary, or to your grandchildren. In the meantime, trust assets may be out of the reach of creditors, divorcing spouses, etc. The same GST tax will apply to this type of bequest, but the same $1.1 million exemption will be available. Best of all, with The Wealth Trust® you decide who gets what and when. You can build an incentive clause and structure a distribution scheme that is consistent with your values and objectives.

While you're creating this type of sophisticated estate plan, don't overlook your IRA or other tax-deferred retirement plans. Such assets won't be affected by whatever you have in your will; instead, they'll pass to beneficiaries you name on a special form for each account.

Often, your spouse will be the designated beneficiary. But if you're not currently married or if your spouse has sufficient assets, you might name a child as the beneficiary of your retirement account. Again, you can name your grandchildren or a trust (as described above) as contingent beneficiaries of your IRA.

After your death, your children will have nine months to decide whether they'll need the IRA. If not, they can disclaim the inherited IRA to a trust, with your grandchildren as trust beneficiaries. The trustee can make sure that distributions are stretched out over your grandchildren's long life expectancies.

Suppose, for example, that your daughter inherits your IRA when she is 59. She can take minimum distributions over a life expectancy of 25 years. On the other hand, if your daughter's son inherits (outright or in trust), at age 23, he will have 59 years to stretch out distributions: an extra 34 years. Unless your daughter truly needs the money in the IRA, it makes sense for her to disclaim in favor of your grandson–and you should have an estate plan in place that will make this all possible.

Again, leaving an IRA to a grandchild will trigger the GST tax but you can use a $1.1 million GST exemption. What's more, these numbers are scheduled to change in the future and there undoubtedly will be further legislation in this area. Therefore, you should work with an advisor who's experienced in wills and trusts, in order to create a flexible plan, and you need to check back with your advisor every few years, to see if your plan needs updating.

Just as important, you need to explain your plan to all the heirs and backup heirs, so they understand what you've done–and what they need to do after you're no longer able to make plans for your loved ones.

SIMPLE AS A-B

One type of trust that's often used for deferring and diminishing estate tax is variously known as a credit shelter trust, bypass trust, or B trust. You may find it simpler to think of this trust as a "family" trust paired with a "marital" trust or an A trust. Married couples create these trusts to take advantage of the unlimited marital deduction from estate tax.

In a basic plan, the family trust holds assets that are passed to the next generation when the first spouse dies. This trust may be funded up to the amount sheltered by an estate tax credit, which is $1.5 million in 2004. Under current law, that amount will increase to $3.5 million by 2009. The decedent's other assets are left to the marital trust.

Because one bequest (family trust) is sheltered by the estate tax credit and the other bequest (marital trust) is sheltered by the unlimited marital deduction, no estate tax is due at the first spouse's death. The surviving spouse is usually named a beneficiary of both trusts.

This process is meant to remove some assets from the reach of estate tax while deferring any estate tax that must be paid to the second spouse's death. At this point, another type of irrevocable trust is used, to hold life insurance. Typically, the trustee will use the life insurance proceeds to buy assets from the estate and the cash can be used by the estate to pay various costs, including estate taxes.

Such a strategy may help heirs pay estate tax without having to liquidate or borrow against valued assets. Then the life insurance trust can liquidate and distribute the assets that have been purchased to the beneficiaries, who usually are the heirs to the estate. Another approach is to have the life insurance trust remain in existence such as The Wealth Trust®, keeping some or all of the assets it has purchased. Then the trust can act as a "family bank," protecting those assets from creditors, divorce actions, and so on, but making distributions to the beneficiaries when they're needed. (For more on estate tax reduction strategies please see Chapter 8).

A/B TRUSTS–BASIC ESTATE PLANNING

1. Estate is valued
2. Estate Tax Return is filed
3. Trust "B" is funded

Husband's Estate
$2,850,000

4. Trust "A" gets funded

$1,500,000 to Husband's Estate Tax Exempt "B" Trust

At the surviving spouse's death, all trust assets, plus all growth passes completely estate tax-free to children

Balance of Husband's Assets, $1,350,000 to "A Trust"

At the surviving spouse's death, Trust A and spouse's assets are subject to estate taxes before going to children

Chapter 3
Setting Priorities

As is the case with anything that's truly important, creating an estate plan should be an exercise in putting first things first. You need to decide where your assets will go: to your spouse, your children, to other loved ones, or to charity.

If you're married, you probably will want to take care of your surviving spouse. Often, though, that may not be easy to do. If you leave assets outright to your surviving spouse, they may reach a point where they can't manage their own affairs. Or, they may be unable to turn down dubious requests for those assets, perhaps from other family members.

Often, the best decision is to leave money to a trust, with your spouse as beneficiary. A reliable trustee may be able to provide necessary funds so that your surviving spouse can live in comfort, yet protect the trust assets from being squandered.

Including a trust in your estate plan is not necessarily the right move in all cases, but you should at least consider creating a trust as a way to meet your goals. Moreover, trusts may be useful for transferring assets to loved ones other than your surviving spouse.

Here are some situations in which the proper use of a trust can help you set priorities:

HOUSE CALLS

Suppose, for example, you have a valuable house or vacation home that you want to keep in the family by passing it to the next generation. How can you transfer that house to your children?

By sale. This tactic will put cash in your pocket. What's more, if it's a principal residence, you won't owe tax on up to $250,000 worth of capital gains ($500,000 if you're married). You can keep living in the house, too, if it's a sale-leaseback.

On the other hand, your children may have to come up with a sizable amount of cash to buy the house from you. Alternatively, they may have to take on a great deal of debt.

Again, your decision should be a matter of priorities. This approach will work best if you need the sales proceeds and you have wealthy, high-income kids who can use the tax advantages of a sale-leaseback.

By gift. Giving away a valuable house will eat into your gift/estate tax exemption. You can, though, give away fractional interests each year, taking valuation discounts to reduce your gift tax exposure.

With careful planning you can keep each gift within the annual gift tax exclusion ($22,000 per married couple per recipient per year) and thus avoid all taxes while removing the house from your taxable estate. If you've given away, say, 40% of the house and then decide to sell it, you'll split the sales proceeds 60-40.

However, expensive paperwork and appraisals may be involved with a series of small, periodic gifts. Therefore, this technique will work best if estate tax reduction is your prime concern and you won't need to tap the equity in the house for your own retirement.

By bequest. Perhaps the simplest approach is to just hold onto the house until your death, or the death of the surviving spouse, and then leave it to your children in a will. They'll inherit with a basis step-up, under current law.

The drawback here is that the house will be included in your taxable estate–under current law, a valuable house may generate hundreds of thousands of dollars in estate tax. Now, though, there is the prospect of estate tax reform or even repeal, so your house might not be subject to estate tax, if you hold onto it.

Generally, this is the "default" option, the plan you'll prefer if you have little worry about estate tax and no special circumstances. You always can sell the house rather than leave it to your kids; a sale may well provide you with tax-free cash.

In trust. Yet another strategy is to leave your house to a trust for your children. This strategy might be preferred if you have children who are minors, incapacitated, likely to be financially irresponsible, or vulnerable to creditors. If your son or daughter gets involved in a messy divorce some day, a house owned outright will be subject to a property settlement but not a house owned by a trust.

As you might suspect, there is a downside here, too. At some point in the future, your children might want to sell an inherited house. If the house is held in trust, such a sale might not qualify for the $250,000 or $500,000 capital gains exclusion.

In situations such as the ones mentioned above, a trust may be the best way to pass on a valuable house. However, if you do create a trust you might want to give the trust beneficiary the power to invade trust principal or to appoint trust principal to another person. This may make the beneficiary the home "owner," eligible for the capital gains exclusion.

SPECIAL CARE FOR SPECIAL NEEDS

Special needs trusts also may fit into estate plans these days. That's especially true for parents of disabled children who are likely to outlive them by a lengthy time period. Such children will need extensive support over the years for customized vans, housing, and so on.

In many cases, special needs trusts are designed to provide beneficiaries with the money necessary for such items yet preserve their eligibility for federal and state programs such as Supplemental Security Income (SSI) and Medicaid. There may be programs that are only open to people who are receiving such public benefits, and people who have a certain amount of assets won't qualify. Properly drafted, special needs trusts can help beneficiaries retain their eligibility for these benefits.

REMARRIAGE VOWS

Among the most complicated estate planning situations are those where a remarriage is involved, particularly where there are children from a previous marriage. A new marriage means taking on new responsibilities even while maintaining existing ones.

If you have children from a previous marriage, you should take steps to protect them, especially if those children are young. It's not realistic to expect a new spouse to have the same loyalties to those children as your former spouse.

Nevertheless, when some people remarry they put all of their assets in joint name with the new spouse or they make wills leaving everything to that spouse. There may be a verbal agreement that the new spouse "will take care of the children" if anything should happen. But that puts the children from the first marriage at risk.

In addition to such joint loyalties, remarried individuals may have to cope with the "long fingers of the first spouse." Especially in the case of a business owner or professional, there's often the presumption, fair or unfair, that the first spouse worked two jobs to carry the breadwinner in the years before success arrived. Then, just when all that sacrifice began to pay off, the first spouse was dumped for another.

In some cases, ex-spouses may ask the courts for additional child support and alimony; courts may be sympathetic if they think the first spouse has been treated unfairly. Joint assets of the second marriage may be awarded to the first spouse, even those that originated from the second spouse.

Therefore, it's vital that the divorce proceedings from the previous marriage be handled properly, with both sides represented by able counsel. That may make it more difficult for an ex-spouse to claim a larger award in later years. Moreover, a prenuptial agreement should be entered into before the remarriage. A valid prenuptial can protect the property of all the parties involved.

The rules on prenuptial agreements vary by state but, in general, such an agreement should list both parties' assets, as of the date of the remarriage. These "sole and separate assets" may be kept separate. Thus, the original owners may be able to claim their individual assets, in case of a subsequent divorce, or direct how they'll be transferred, as part of an estate plan. In order for a prenuptial to be recognized by a court, both sides should have independent counsel and the agreement should not be one-sided.

A problem may arise if one spouse's assets appreciate during the marriage. Suppose a business owner's company doubles in value during the five years of a remarriage, and then that marriage ends in divorce. How will that appreciation be divided? Such questions should be addressed in the prenuptial agreement.

Moreover, a prenuptial agreement should be coordinated with your will, any trust documents, and other elements of your estate plan. You don't want your will to leave certain assets to your children while those same assets are given to your new spouse, as part of a prenuptial agreement.

Of course, asking a spouse-to-be to provide a list of assets, for a prenuptial agreement, isn't the most romantic topic of conversation for a couple making marriage plans. One tactic is to tell your prospective spouse that you're revising your entire estate plan–which you should be doing. That estate plan might include a prenuptial along with a new will, trusts, etc.

Another approach is to tell your spouse that you have an adviser, such as an accountant or a financial planner, who insists that you have a prenuptial agreement in place before the remarriage. Blame anyone you want—but just make sure you get it done.

Besides drawing up a new will and creating a prenuptial, what else needs to be done before a remarriage? You should update your beneficiary designations. You probably have life insurance and retirement plans; make sure the proceeds will go to the proper parties at your death.

Retirement plans may be particularly important assets for many people. Spouses are entitled to be the beneficiaries of employer-sponsored plans, unless those rights are waived. If you intend to designate someone besides your spouse, such as a child from a previous marriage, as a retirement plan beneficiary, there are some hurdles to clear. A spouse may only waive a spouse's rights, so such a waiver can't be included in a prenuptial agreement. A prenuptial agreement might include a promise that such rights will be waived after the marriage. Penalties can be established, in the prenuptial agreement, in case of failure to fulfill such a promise.

If you have children from a previous marriage, you may want to take steps to see that they have assets of their own. You can put money into custodial accounts but such funds go to the children outright after the children come of age, so there's a lack of long-term control. If substantial assets are involved, you can set up a trust and name the children as beneficiaries. You probably should not name your second spouse as trustee, though.

Be careful how property is titled: holding assets in joint name with your spouse may win you points at home but will cost you flexibility. That is, all jointly held property automatically will go to your spouse if you're the first to die, no matter what it says in your will. If you transfer your brokerage account into joint name, for example, all of those securities will pass to your spouse and not to your children.

In such circumstances life insurance may be a great equalizer. Regardless of how property is titled, your estate plan probably will call for substantial assets to go your spouse. By buying life insurance and naming children from a previous marriage as beneficiaries, you can be sure that they, too, will receive a significant inheritance.

Besides taking care of children from a previous marriage, you also should decide where you will live after the remarriage: in a home that the bride or the groom already owns or in a different one. Often, a remarrying couple will sell one or even two homes. If that's the case, it's probably better to wait until after the marriage to make the sale. That's because a married homeowner can claim a $500,000 capital gain exclusion on the sale of a principal residence while a single homeowner can exclude only $250,000 worth of gain. With all the talk about the "marriage penalty" that taxpayers face, you might as well take advantage of such a sizable wedding gift from the IRS.

POST-MORTEM MOTIVATION

As mentioned before, sophisticated estate planning goes beyond minimizing the amount lost in taxes and maximizing the amount passed on to heirs. Many wealthy individuals are concerned about leaving too much to children, grandchildren, and even great-grandchildren–they're concerned about spoiling them and making life too easy.

To avoid providing disincentives to heirs, you can provide the right incentives in the form of an incentive trust, also known as a family incentive trust. In some ways, creating such a trust contradicts traditional estate planning. Often, people who are concerned about how their heirs will handle money create a trust with restrictions, limiting access to income or principal. An incentive trust, on the other hand, is designed to provide rewards for behavior the grantor favors.

Many wealthy individuals are afraid that their heirs won't work if they inherit a great deal of money. They don't want their heirs to become like the English landed gentry of a few centuries ago, who lost all incentive to lead productive lives. For such people, estate tax saving is a secondary concern: they are more interested in the effective disposition of their assets. That's where an incentive trust can help.

Individuals who set up these trusts might act at a time when their own children are grown and established in their own careers. They've seen that their kids are okay but they don't know about their grandchildren, who are still minors. Thus, they might give their children a limited power of appointment.

That is, the children can't distribute assets to themselves but they can set terms for distributions to the next generation. In some cases, the trust creator's children may be able to set new incentives for grandchildren or great-grandchildren. You don't know what the future might bring so you may want to permit some ability to adapt to changing circumstances.

In other situations, the kids are already ruined, in the eyes of their parents, who have spoiled them. Grandparents don't want the same thing for their grandchildren: they want these grandchildren to be well adjusted, to act with honesty and integrity. In pursuit of those lofty goals, they may turn to a family incentive trust.

A typical incentive trust has three aspects.

- First is a safety net. Certain provisions are designed to ensure that the trust beneficiaries won't be destitute; they'll be provided with whatever is necessary for education, medical care, and long-term care.
- Second is an income component. There might be some provision to match earned income. Thus, the trust will be structured so that nobody will be able to live solely from the trust fund.

  Income matching programs generally are aimed at young people, perhaps up to age 30. For example, the trustee might be instructed to pay 10% to 30% of a trust beneficiary's earned income. If a teenager earns $4,000 from a summer job, the trustee might provide another $400 to $1,200. The idea is to encourage young people to develop good work habits.

  Will this encourage some trust beneficiaries to take up careers that are more financially rewarding but not as beneficial to society? A grandchild who might have considered teaching elementary school may be tempted to become a corporate raider instead, lured by the trust fund match.

  Nevertheless, the family incentive trust can be structured to deal with such concerns. The amount of earned income qualifying for a match might be capped. The idea is to induce trust beneficiaries to work, not to seek certain high-paying jobs.

- Third, trust incentives can be tailored to encourage socially desirable goals. For example, some trusts might include a "family Nobel prize." Every five years or so, a panel of independent parties might choose the trust beneficiary that has made the greatest contribution to society, and a sizable amount of money may be awarded. This can help to reward beneficiaries whose careers don't pay as much.

SEED MONEY

Other types of incentives might call for independent guidance, too. Some incentive trusts are structured to help beneficiaries start a business; if so, an outside administrator, chosen by the trustee, might be called upon to approve a business plan and recommend a cash distribution from the trust. The trustee would have to approve, too, providing a "double negative" before money will be advanced.

With such provisions, incentive trusts can act as a family venture capital firm. One of your descendants may eventually create a business worth $100 million or $1 billion, thanks to your $1 million that started it all.

Trust incentives can go far beyond income matching and business startups to advanced education, housing down payments, and more. In essence, incentives can encourage any type of behavior that you feel is important.

Suppose, for example, that you are extremely opposed to parents putting young children in day care; your trust might provide a substantial amount of money, indexed to inflation, for parents who stay at home with their children. Alternatively, you might create a cash incentive for those who become missionaries in third-world countries.

It's important to structure the incentives so that trust beneficiaries are well motivated to succeed on their own. You might stipulate that the trustee will provide money for a down payment on a first house, but only if the beneficiary can qualify to carry the mortgage on that house.

Similar provisions might apply to a business startup. The trust might make funding of a new business contingent on attracting debt or equity financing from an outside source. In addition, there might be a provision that a beneficiary can't receive money for a business startup more than once every two years, or as long as five years. That will prevent a beneficiary from starting a new business each year, going bankrupt, and coming back for more.

Often, you'll be relying upon the trustee to make the appropriate distribution. Indeed, many incentive trusts are "dynasty trusts," designed to serve multiple generations, so some mechanism must be in place for successor trustees to be named. You probably should include a trustee removal power, too, to protect future trust beneficiaries from an unsatisfactory trustee. If, say, 75% or 80% of the beneficiaries agree, the trustee can be replaced.

With an incentive trust, you should have a plan for building up the trust as much as possible so there will be enough money available to meet future needs of the beneficiaries. One approach is to have each family member buy life insurance to augment the investment pool. Generation after generation, this keeps building the trust fund.

If you are going to set up an incentive trust, the matter should be explained to other family members. Explain to the children you're doing this for their protection; assets held in the trust will be out of the reach of creditors and estate tax while the trustee will have the flexibility to provide for the beneficiaries.

LEARNING CURVE

For most people, a top priority is seeing that children and grandchildren receive an excellent education. The federal government has provided some help: under the Economic Growth and Tax Relief Reconciliation Act of 2001 (EGTRRA), Section 529 plans are now income-tax free, if the proceeds are used for higher education.

Moreover, these plans also offer gift and estate tax benefits. Money contributed to a 529 account is considered a gift, the same as if you make a deposit in a youngster's custodial account. Contributions to 529 plans are considered present interests, so they're eligible for the annual gift tax exclusion. Currently, you can give away up to $11,000 worth of assets to any number of recipients, tax-free, because of this exclusion; for married couples, the limit is $22,000 per recipient. See detailed discussion in Chapter 4.)

What's more, special tax rules apply to 529 accounts. You can make up to five years' worth of gifts upfront. Gifts in excess of $11,000 or $22,000 can be spread over more than one year, if you make an election on a gift tax return.

For example, Jim and Joan Smith can put $110,000 into a 529 plan for their daughter Ashley this year, tax-free, if they elect to spread this gift over five years. They must file gift tax returns each year to complete the transaction. If the account owner dies before the fifth year, a portion of the gift would come back into the taxable estate.

What are the advantages of this tactic? You can move a large amount of money out of your estate, without owing tax. Any appreciation is removed from the estate, too.

Nevertheless, account owners still exercise considerable control over assets that have been moved beyond the reach of estate tax. You can shift funds among different 529 plans, change the beneficiary to another family member, and even take the money back, if needed, although you'll have to pay tax and a 10% penalty on any earnings. There are few other opportunities for reducing estate tax yet retaining control.

Control might be even more than the wealth reclamation opportunity. Even if you are not necessarily concerned about getting your money back, you might like the idea that you will have a say in how the money will be spent. If one beneficiary turns out to be a ne'er-do-well, you can change the beneficiary to some other relative.

WHEN 529 PLANS FLUNK THE TEST

With all of these advantages, though, there may be a downside to making large contributions to 529 plans. There could be disadvantages for purposes of creditor protection, Medicaid planning, divorce, etc. Such issues may vary, state by state, but it's possible that other types of transfers will offer more benefits in these areas.

In addition, you might not want to use up your annual gift tax exclusions on 529 contributions. Minority interests in real estate or a family business may be transferred at a valuation discount; using a family limited partnership (FLP) or a limited liability company (LLC) might increase the size of that discount. You may prefer to transfer $15,000 or $16,000 worth of assets, via an FLP or an LLC, rather than remove $11,000 from your estate with a 529 contribution.

Thus, for the very wealthy, or those who feel they can make consistent annual exclusion gifts, gifts of highly discounted assets such as stock in a closely held business may be preferable to contributing to a 529 plan. However, if there are no family business shares or similar discounted interests or a regular program of gifting to transfer, 529 plans may be ideal for making gifts because of the income tax benefits.

If you are already in the practice of making estate-reduction gifts, there may not be much annual exclusion left to shelter 529 contributions. In such a scenario, you can still use the "Section 2503(e) exclusion," which permits people to make direct tuition payments for someone else, free of gift tax. Indeed, you might want to make both 529 contributions and tax-free tuition payments, to maximize gifting opportunities.

Moreover, multiple 529 accounts might be used to help resolve problems with the annual gift tax exclusion. Suppose you wish to contribute $11,000 to a 529 account for a child but have only $4,000 of gift tax exclusion remaining for the year, because of other gifts to the same child in the same year. You could use the five-year averaging election described above to make a full $11,000 gift.

Alternatively, you may decide to contribute $4,000 to a 529 account for this child, which will be covered by the gift tax exclusion, and another $6,000 into a 529 account where you name yourself as the beneficiary. In a later year, if there is unused gift tax exclusion, funds may be transferred from the self-beneficiary account to the child-beneficiary account. In the meantime, the entire $11,000 will be in a tax-free 529 environment.

Such gift-tax strategies are aimed at reducing a future estate tax, which may not be an issue, now that the estate tax exemption is scheduled to increase (at least temporarily) and outright repeal is a possibility. Regardless of what happens to estate tax legislation, though, it's probable that some people will accumulate large sums in 529 accounts. In 2003, for example, loving grandparents could give away a total of $880,000, if they have eight grandchildren. An asset of that magnitude merits careful estate planning.

To begin with, one person usually holds title to a 529 account because joint ownership is not permitted. Most plans permit the account holder to designate a backup who'll take over in case of death or incapacity, so you should name a replacement.

If no successor is listed, and the account holder dies, the former owner's executor will become the new account holder. Generally, a new account holder will have the same powers over the account, unless constrained by a letter of intent filed with the 529 plan. The powers of a successor account holder may be greater or smaller, depending on plan specifics. With some plans, for example, if a child inherits a 529 account, that new owner could divide the account among more than one of his or her own children.

If an account holder becomes incapacitated and no successor has been named, control of the 529 accounts likely will pass to a guardian or the holder of a power of attorney. For that reason, your durable power of attorney should specifically permit gifts to 529 plans. In particular, five-year front-loading should be allowed. Many powers of attorney limit gifts to $11,000, the maximum for tax-free gifts in prior years, and those gifts may only be made to family members.

BREAKING EVEN

Additional language may be necessary to precisely spell out a power of attorney's power over 529 plans. For example, suppose your son has five children, your daughter has one child, and the power of attorney permits maximum five-year 529 front-loading. Do you want an equalization provision to prevent your son's side of the family getting so much more than your daughter's side or would you want each grandchild to receive the same amount for higher education?

Many estate planning issues relating to 529 plans are dependent on state law. In some states, for example, 529 accounts are subject to prenuptial agreements, divisible in marital settlements, or protected from creditors. Treatment of these funds probably will evolve as 529 plans grow in importance but for now these are issues you should consider when planning for a large 529 account.

What's more, federal law permits 529 accounts to be owned by "person," which could include a corporation or a trust. The language of each state's plan will determine whether a trust or a corporation actually may hold an account.

Why name a trust as owner of a 529 account? Section 529 plans can be superb but they are still relatively new in the scheme of estate planning and the kinks have yet to be worked out. Especially for non-traditional families, very wealthy families, and couples considering divorce, care should be exercised and a trust may be better for the flexibility it provides. A trust can be preferable when it comes to maintaining a succession plan, compared with the usual practice of naming an individual successor as account owner.

For instance, people in uncertain marriages may prefer to keep 529 accounts in trust. In the event of a divorce, it may be better to hold the account in trust rather than "trusting" an ex-spouse as account owner. That is, if a 529 account is held in a trust, it may not be subject to a property settlement. A trustee of your choice can see that the terms of the trust are followed; probably to make certain that the money is spent on higher education. If the account is awarded to an ex-spouse in a divorce settlement, it may be terminated.

Recently, IRAs and other tax-deferred retirement plans have become the subjects of intensive estate planning. In some ways, 529 plans are similar to IRAs: they offer income tax advantages, they're not covered by the owner's will, they can bypass probate with a successor designation, and in some situations it makes sense to name a trust to succeed the account owner.

Just as a thorough estate strategy for a retirement plan can generate huge benefits, so can a thoughtful estate plan for a 529 plan. Indeed, you might want to consider an "educational endowment," which can be likened to a stretch IRA.

Some money contributed to a 529 plan might not be spent on higher education within a few years. Unused funds can grow tax-free, for decades, as new beneficiaries are named. Given certain assumptions, the buildup can be extraordinary. An example from the MFS family of mutual funds shows a $110,000 contribution growing to more than $1.3 million in 50 years, even after paying to send a child and two grandchildren through four years of college.

The money that's been "banked" in this manner might be available for all types of accredited higher education, over the years, and even for non-educational purposes, if taxes and penalties are paid. There might be problems with the generation-skipping transfer tax but the future of that tax, along with the estate tax, is impossible to predict, so 529 contributions might be cultivated into your family's private scholarship fund.

SWEET CHARITY

While you're setting your priorities in your estate plan, you probably will want to "give something back" by contributing to your favorite causes. Generally, when making charitable contributions during your lifetime you're better off giving away appreciated assets instead of cash. You'll receive tax deductions based on the full value of the donated assets while the accrued capital gains tax obligation disappears.

Moreover, giving away such assets allows you to hold onto your IRA and other tax-deferred retirement accounts as long as possible. The longer income tax can be deferred, the greater the wealth that builds inside the plan and the larger the ultimate payout to you and your family.

This strategy works fine–as long as you're alive. When it comes to estate planning, though, you should shift into reverse. That is, for charitable bequests, you should use your IRAs or qualified plans. At the same time, leave your appreciated stocks and mutual fund shares to your heirs.

Suppose, for example, you're unmarried (widowed or divorced) with total assets of $2 million: $1 million in an IRA and $1 million in appreciated stocks and real estate. You want to leave $1 million to your children and $1 million to your alma mater.

Because you're making a $1 million charitable bequest, no estate tax will be due. This gift will be deducted from your taxable estate, reducing it to $1 million, below the estate-tax threshold in effect during 2004.

Income taxes, though, are another story. If the appreciated assets are left to charity while the IRA goes to relatives, your heirs eventually will have to pay income tax on all the money as it comes out of the IRA. Assuming a 40% effective tax rate, your heirs will inherit an IRA worth $600,000, not $1 million.

Instead, suppose you leave your IRA to charity and bequeath the appreciated assets to your children. Again, there will be no estate tax.

Under current law, though, your children will inherit the appreciated assets with a "step-up in basis." That means they inherit assets worth a full $1 million: they can sell those assets and not owe any capital gains tax on appreciation during your lifetime.

The bottom line: this approach—IRA to charity and appreciated assets to loved ones—can pass on such an estate completely tax-free, saving hundreds of thousands of dollars in taxes. Larger estates may owe estate tax but the principle is the same: your family can avoid paying deferred income tax if you leave IRA funds to charity.

In reality, if you have a $1 million IRA you probably would want to leave $10,000 or $50,000 or $100,000 to charity rather than the entire amount. That used to be a tricky process because income tax complications could arise. Fortunately, this issue has been clarified.

Under IRS regulations issued in 2002, a charitable beneficiary can be cashed out while the other beneficiaries stretch out minimum required distributions. Suppose you have a $1 million IRA and you want to leave $250,000 to a particular charity. You can specify that $250,000 bequest on the beneficiary designation form—most forms have enough room for this type of arrangement. If not, you can attach a separate sheet to the form. After your death, your heirs will have until September 30th of the following year to pay $250,000 from the IRA to the charity. The balance of the IRA can be paid out over the life expectancies of the other beneficiaries.

One or two specified charities can be designated as IRA beneficiaries. Often, though, Private Foundations and donor-advised funds are named as the beneficiaries. Parents might see these entities as vehicles for bringing the children together in the future, even if they wind up in different places. The idea is that the family members will meet; one or more times a year, to make the decisions about charitable contributions.

As a rule of thumb, it takes funding of $1 million or more to make setting up a Private Foundation worthwhile, considering the administration and reporting requirements. For smaller amounts, donor-advised funds can make sense.

Regardless of whether a Private Foundation or a donor-advised fund is designated as an IRA beneficiary, either can be created sooner, to provide immediate tax benefits. One approach is to create a Charitable Lead Trust to fund a Private Foundation or donor-advised fund right away. The trust assets can go to the children eventually, with minimal gift and estate tax consequences. At the same time, a Charitable Remainder Trust can be set up to provide income to the donor or family members upfront, with the trust assets going to the Private Foundation or donor-advised fund in the future. With such innovative planning, you can have charitable donations coming and going, enjoying multiple tax benefits along the way.

SPOUSE CALLS

Making charitable bequests from your IRA is fairly simple if you're single. However, you may face a conflict if you're married and you'd like your IRA to provide for your surviving spouse as well as for your favorite causes.

Unless the bequest is relatively small in relation to your entire estate, your surviving spouse won't want to give up your IRA. In this situation, what are your options?

- Leave your IRA to your spouse, who can leave the IRA to charity at the second death.

  You can name your spouse as primary beneficiary and a charity as contingent beneficiary. Your spouse can disclaim all or part of the IRA, which would then go to the charity.

  This approach offers flexibility. To make it work, though, your spouse must be able to handle the IRA wisely, while aging, and make the charitable bequest you desire.

- Leave your IRA to a QTIP (Qualified Terminable Interest Property) trust. QTIPs give the surviving spouse all the trust income for life while the first spouse to die gets to name the ultimate beneficiary—in this case, a charity.

  Thus, all payouts from the IRA will go to the surviving spouse, who'll pay income tax. In case of need, the trustee can distribute more funds to the survivor. At the second death, the money left in the IRA goes to the charity named by the first spouse to die, and further income tax is avoided.

  The catch? Your surviving spouse might live so long that most or all of your IRA will be paid out, leaving little or nothing to charity. This problem is unique to situations where an IRA is left to a QTIP, as the measuring life expectancy for your surviving spouse is calculated at her actual life expectancy, not at the more favorable new Uniform Table.

- Leave your IRA to a Charitable Remainder Trust (CRT) and name your spouse as income beneficiary. This can limit the surviving spouse's income to, say, 8% of trust assets per year assuring that there will be a trust fund to eventually pass to charity.

  You can provide your spouse with some other percentage of the trust fund each year, with a 5% minimum. Whatever you decide, you'll put a limit on the survivor's income and assure a future charitable gift.

- Life insurance to charity. You may buy a policy and deduct premiums annually. Utilize a limited pay guaranteed policy to protect the charity.

Chapter 4
Sooner Than Later

The idea of "estate planning" may lead you to think of actions that will take place after your death. That's when you will leave an estate, which you'd like to distribute to various relatives, friends, and charities.

In truth, estate planning can begin during your lifetime, if you give away your assets. That way, you can be sure your possessions will wind up in the right hands. If you give away your family's silverware to your daughter, for example, you'll be able to see her enjoying those treasured items–you might even be served a meal at her home and use the utensils yourself!

As is often the case in estate planning, though, taxes play a crucial role. After all, what's to stop you from giving away a $10 million estate and leaving yourself no estate to tax, at your death?

The federal gift tax serves this purpose. You can't reduce estate tax by simply giving away assets, because the gift tax will be triggered.

For years, federal gift and estate taxes have been unified. However, the 2001 tax law sunders this relationship. While the estate tax exemption equivalent gradually increases from $1 million in 2003 to $3.5 million in 2009 to total repeal in 2010, the gift tax does not follow the same path. The amount each person can give away, tax-free, increased from $675,000 to $1 million in 2002–and then stopped. No further increases are scheduled; neither is repeal of the gift tax. It truly is a system where you have to "die to win."

Fortunately, the annual gift tax exclusion was not affected by this law. Therefore, it will become increasingly important to use this exclusion as a means of reducing a taxable estate.

As the name suggests, the gift tax exclusion permits you to give away assets without paying a gift tax. Also, gifts covered by this exclusion won't have estate tax consequences.

For years, the gift tax exclusion had been $10,000 per recipient per year. A tax law passed in 1997 indexes the exclusion in $1,000 increments, so the limit was raised to $11,000 in 2002 and will gradually keep increasing to $12,000, $13,000, etc.

For now, the $11,000 exclusion provides ample opportunities. Suppose you have two sons, two beloved daughters-in-law, and four adored grandchildren. You can give each of these eight individuals up to $11,000 worth of assets every year. This would remove $88,000 worth of assets from your taxable estate, as well as future income and future appreciation of those assets.

You don't even have to file a gift tax return for such gifts. However, these gifts are "use it or lose it." If you neglected to use the exclusion in 2003, for example, you can't double up in 2004.

Married couples can each give up to $11,000 per recipient per year, for a total of $22,000. What's more, married couples can agree to split gifts.

Suppose, in the above example, you're remarried. Naturally, your new spouse won't want to give your family members $88,000 per year. However, you can give away $176,000 of your own funds ($22,000 to each of eight recipients) without tax consequences.

To do so, your spouse must formally agree to the transaction: a signature on a gift tax return is required. In this case, your spouse can make no gifts that year to those beneficiaries under the gift tax exclusion.

If you decide to use the gift tax exclusion, what should you give away? Cash is simplest. There are no worries about valuation or basis while all the income generated by that cash, in the future, won't generate an income tax for you and won't wind up in your taxable estate.

You might not have tens of thousands of dollars in cash to give away each year, though. Therefore, you may choose to give away stocks, mutual fund shares, or other publicly traded securities.

Again, giving such assets avoids valuation problems. If you give your son 200 shares of Microsoft when they're trading at $55, that's an $11,000 gift.

However, such a gift also transfers your cost basis in the stock. If your basis is $40 per share, that basis carries over to your son. If he eventually sells Microsoft at $75, he'll owe tax on a $35 per-share gain, not $20 per share.

Therefore, the best strategy may be to give away shares with only a slight appreciation, because you're giving away only a slight tax obligation. Don't give away shares held at a loss; instead, sell them first to reap the tax benefit and then give away the cash.

Giveaways of appreciated securities may be especially helpful if you have college age or college bound children and you need to sell those securities to pay for their education. You and your spouse can give each child up to $22,000 worth of these securities each year, tax-free, and your children can sell the shares.

As long as your children are 14 or older, they'll probably pay tax at a 10% rate rather than your higher rate. If they sell assets that have been held longer than five years, taxes will be owed at an even lower 8% rate.

In addition, you might give away illiquid assets such as shares in a family business. Vehicles such as Family Limited Partnerships (FLPs) and Limited Liability Companies (LLCs) often are used, to extend the tax benefits, but care must be taken, as explained below.

PRESENT TENSE

As mentioned, the $1 million lifetime cap on the gift-tax exemption makes the use of the annual gift tax exclusion more important. However, it's vital that such gifts represent a "present interest" in the transferred assets. Without a present interest, the annual gift tax exclusion won't apply and you might owe gift tax.

That trap snared Albert and Christine Hackl, who purchased land to be planted for tree farms. They contributed the land, as well as cash and securities, to an LLC, which planted millions of trees.

The Hackls made gifts of LLC units to over 40 different family members, including their eight children and the children's spouses. These gifts were made up to the limits of the annual gift tax exclusion and the Hackls claimed that all the gifts qualified for this exclusion.

Within three years, the gift recipients owned 51% of the LLC interests but no gift tax had been paid. The IRS balked, asserting that the gifts did not qualify for the exclusion, and assessed a gift tax liability of over $600,000.

In 2002, the Tax Court ruled in favor of the IRS. According to the court, there were too many restrictions on the recipients. The underlying asset was young timberland, with no prospect of income any time soon, and there were barriers to transfers. The recipients of the gifts couldn't withdraw any money, compel distributions, or sell their interests to outsiders without the manager's approval. Albert Hackl, as manager of the LLC, had retained complete control.

As the court reasoned, the tree farms were not likely to produce any income in the next few years. Moreover, if and when income is generated, the gift recipients will get distributions only if the manager decides to make a payout. Thus, any benefit from the transferred interests will come in the future, not in the present. Without a present interest, the annual gift tax exclusions did not apply and all the transfers were subject to gift tax.

The implication? If you are relying upon the annual gift tax exclusion for estate reduction, be sure that your gifts qualify as present interests. Recipients must be entitled to immediately benefit from the assets they've been given, through possession or enjoyment or income generation. If the recipient's benefits from the property will come in the future, no gift tax exclusion will be permitted.

To sustain the annual gift tax exclusions, in the case of a closely held company, you might make cash distributions regularly to all shareholders, including the ones who have been given interests. Many family businesses, however, will not want to make substantial cash distributions to all shareholders. Other assets, such as undeveloped land, do not generate income.

Thus, cash distributions may be impossible or impractical. If so, owners of transferred interests might get other benefits. Such benefits could include the right to demand distributions or the right to sell their shares at a fair market value, back to the other owners. If your beneficiaries have such rights you'll have a much better chance of sustaining the annual gift tax exclusion, even if those rights are seldom actually exercised.

In any case, you may want to file a gift tax return for all transfers to younger family members, even though such a filing may not be required, if the annual gift tax exclusion applies. Under current law, the IRS has three years after a gift tax return is filed, to raise any legal or factual issues. If no challenge is filed in that time period, and all the information was adequately disclosed, the exclusions will be upheld.

Under prior law, the IRS could wait until you died, then examine all of your lifetime gifts when it audited your estate tax return. If that estate tax audit takes place, say, in the year 2042, it might be difficult for your executor to demonstrate that the building you gave to your kids in 2002 really was worth $300,000. Depending on future estate tax law, putting an extra $100,000 worth of value on the property, with 40 years' worth of interest and possibly penalties, compounded, could lead to a huge tax bill.

Thanks to the recent change in the law, described above, that threat has been removed. If you get by the three-year limit, your heirs can avoid a challenge far in the future.

STRINGS ATTACHED

In prior years, estate planning not only called for making gifts that would use up your lifetime exemption, you also may have been advised to make taxable gifts. The way the math worked, passing on assets via lifetime gifts is more efficient than making bequests, even if gift tax must be paid.

Such strategies have become less common. Few people are willing to pay gift taxes now, while there is a possibility that the estate tax will be repealed. Moreover, you may be reluctant to give away assets you might need some day. The bear market that began in 2000 has reduced many individuals' net worth and raised fears about the future.

For all of the above reasons, then, lifetime gifts to heirs are less attractive today than they were a few years ago. Instead of gifts to your children, you might prefer to make loans. With loans, you can help your children now, if they need the funds. If you need the money some day, you can get those funds back, from loan repayments. Alternatively, if the economy and stock market turn up in the future, you may be able to make gifts to your children, which the children can use to pay down the loans.

Certain formalities should be followed so that the IRS doesn't treat intra-family loans as gifts. A loan is subject to rules requiring that a minimum interest rate generally be charged. In today's low-interest-rate climate, that rate can be modest.

A short-term loan, for example, might have interest around 2%. If your children or grandchildren can earn more than that, they're ahead of the game. The interest that's paid by your children may be deductible as investment interest while the loans aren't subject to gift or generation-skipping transfer tax. However, if the interest is accrued or rolled up into the principal, these transfers might be treated as gifts rather than loans.

CRUMMEY IDEA

If you decide to make lifetime gifts to younger family members, you may prefer to avoid outright gifts. By making gifts in trust, instead, you reduce the risk that those assets will be squandered. Also, gifts in trust may be required for certain estate planning strategies, such as providing money for a trust to pay life insurance premiums.

The challenge, in these situations, is to get your money into the trust without incurring any gift tax. Ordinarily, a gift to a trust does not qualify for the $11,000-per-recipient annual gift tax exclusion because it does not provide a present interest. However, over the past three decades a technique has evolved for making tax-excludable gifts to trusts.

In essence, after cash is given to the trust, the beneficiaries are sent a letter (a "Crummey notice," named after a landmark court case) by the trustee, informing them of their ability to pull out the money within a certain time period. After that ability lapses, the trustee can use the money for certain purposes or just hold onto it.

By going through this exercise, gifts can qualify for the annual exclusion. If a trust has two beneficiaries, for example, you can transfer up to $22,000 per year to the trust this way, free of gift tax (assuming no other gifts are made to those beneficiaries). A married couple can give $22,000 per trust beneficiary, tax-free. If necessary, one spouse can give money to the other and they both can make gifts to the trust, in order to fully utilize the couple's annual gift tax exclusion.

LIMITED EDITIONS

Sometimes gifts are not made outright or in trust but instead through FLPs and LLCs. The FLP first gained prominence as a technique for separating ownership and control, for estate tax purposes. You can transfer assets to an FLP and then give away limited partnership interests to younger relatives, effectively removing those assets from your taxable estate. Yet you can retain control of those assets through ownership of a general partnership interest.

In the 1990s, rulings by the IRS and the courts confirmed the availability of valuation discounts for those transfers, a development that greatly expanded the popularity of FLPs. Assets worth, say, $1 million can be given away but those assets might be valued at only $600,000 or $700,000 if held within an FLP and subject to liquidity constraints. Similar discounts may result if you use an LLC.

Many IRS challenges to valuation discounts have been rejected by courts so valuation discounts for FLP and LLC transfers are permitted–the question is how large the discount can be, and that's decided on a case-by-case basis. The more qualified your appraiser, the better the chances of prevailing.

Under the 2001 tax law, which caps the lifetime gift tax exemption at $1 million, FLPs and LLCs may be used to get valuation discounts for estate tax as well as gift tax. Even if $1 million worth of assets are transferred during your lifetime ($2 million for a married couple), using up your lifetime gift tax exemption, more assets can be left to the next generation, at your death. Such a bequest may be sheltered by the estate tax exemption, which will be larger than the gift tax exemption, beginning in 2004.

If the interests that are held by the estate makes up a minority of the entity, further discounts may be available. Suppose, for example, you and your spouse form an LLC to hold assets and divide the interests 50-50. During your lifetimes, you and your spouse can give away some of those assets, which may qualify for valuation discounts.

Suppose, at the first spouse's death, each spouse still holds 40% of the LLC. Rather than make an outright bequest to the surviving spouse, that 40% might be left to a QTIP (Qualifying Terminal Interest Property) trust. Such a trust will pay all income to the survivor and provide access to the principal.

When the survivor dies, both the 40% interest in the LLC that's held outright and the 40% held in trust can pass to the next generation. Courts have held that both of these interests qualify for a minority discount—they are not required to be aggregated into one majority holding.

LEARNING TO LOVE AN LLC

As the above example indicates, some estate plans use LLCs rather than FLPs, at least in selected situations. Limited Liability Companies have emerged in recent years as favored structures for small businesses because they offer partnership taxation (no corporate income tax obligations), limited liability for participants, and a means to avoid S corporation requirements.

Increasingly, the LLC is being used instead of an FLP if creditor protection is important. You even can have a one-person LLC to isolate a particular asset. Harry Evans, for example, owns apartment buildings and he uses a separate LLC for each one. If something goes wrong with one property, the problem won't spill over to the others.

On the other hand, an FLP may be preferable to an LLC for assets such as securities. There may not be limited liability issues and the restrictions that come with a limited partnership may provide for larger valuation discounts when the securities are transferred.

Weighing such tradeoffs, LLCs may be selected as the vehicle for holding family assets. When LLCs are used as alternatives for FLPs, it's common for one or two members to be designated as managers. Often, this enables you and your spouse to retain control of the assets held in the LLC, even after those assets have been transferred from your estate. In some situations, though, the desire to retain control can cost tax advantages, as was the case in the Tax Court's recent Hackl decision, described previously.

On the other hand, there's also a bright side to the Hackl decision. The Tax Court said that the interests being transferred lacked liquidity, so they were not eligible for the annual gift tax exclusion. That same reasoning can be used to support the valuation discounts that are claimed, when assets held in FLPs or LLCs are transferred.

Thus, tax advantages are available through the use of FLPs and LLCs. But tax advantages aren't the only reason that you might want to consider these entities. They offer substantial non-tax benefits as well. Using an FLP or an LLC may allow your family to consolidate assets for more effective management, make gifts, and insulate the assets from creditors. In addition, younger family members may become familiar with these assets, as limited partners or non-managing members, and thus become better prepared for future responsibilities.

Such non-tax reasons may make an FLP or an LLC an excellent way to hold real estate. If several people own a property outright, and one wants to sell his or her interest, the result can be a recipe for disaster. By contrast, an FLP or an LLC can be an ideal vehicle ownership of real estate such as a family compound. As many as three generations of the same family might get together to plan a property's future. Agreements can be structured so interests can't be held outside the entity and ownership isn't diffused. For example, restrictions may be placed on the transfer of any interest to a creditor, including a divorcing spouse, of a party to the FLP or LLC. Such transfers may be subject to a right of first refusal by the entity, the other parties, or both.

Holding real estate such as a family compound in an FLP or an LLC can serve significant business purposes. Those include providing centralized management and thereby avoiding deadlock issues, keeping the property intact and in the family, the elimination of any partition rights, the protection of the underlying assets from claims of creditors, and protection of the parties to the FLP or LLC from liability claims of, for example, persons injured on the underlying property.

For some or all of these reasons, as well as tax benefits, you may want to transfer real estate and other assets to heirs using an FLP or LLC. Assuming that very large estates will continue to be taxed, setting up these entities and transferring some assets at a discount, is a way to hedge against future gift and estate taxes.

PIGS GET SLAUGHTERED

As mentioned, the FLP has become a prime estate planning tool, helped in part by some favorable court decisions. In 2002, though, the Estate of Harper case went against the taxpayer. Thus, you have some idea of what you can't do with an FLP.

The Tax Court basically said you're going too far. If you want the tax benefits of the FLP, you need to follow the procedures set forth in the FLP documents and do so in a businesslike manner.

In this case, Morton Harper set up an FLP and funded it with over $1.6 million in cash and securities held in his revocable trust. In a typical FLP, he would have retained a 1% general partnership interest, allowing him to make all the management decisions.

Here, his son (0.4%) and his daughter (0.6%) held a 1% general partnership interest. His son, the managing general partner, was ostensibly in control. However, the general partners faced a laundry list of things they couldn't do without the limited partner's (Morton Harper's) approval, such as trade 5% or more of the portfolio.

Moreover, Harper failed to document how the children acquired their 1% general partnership interest in the first place. There wasn't anything to show what, if anything, the children contributed in exchange for this interest. Harper never filed a gift tax return, for example.

Similarly, Harper was slow to document his own contributions. The agreement referred to Harper's contribution of his "portfolio" but he didn't document any contributions until eight months after the date of the partnership agreement and he didn't finish transferring his property for another three months. He also delayed applying for an employer identification number and he never opened a bank account for the FLP.

Harper died approximately a year after setting up the FLP. During the three months preceding his death and for nine months after his death, the FLP made various distributions that bore no relationship to the partners' respective interests. The partners' ownership interests and capital accounts were not adjusted to reflect these sporadic distributions. The money just went from the assets in the FLP to the bank account of Harper's revocable trust, and then (during his lifetime) to Harper.

According to the Tax Court, this entire exercise was a sham, designed to accomplish nothing but move the assets from Harper's taxable estate.

He maintained control over all of the FLP assets and continued to enjoy access to the income that was generated. Therefore, all of the assets were subject to estate tax so Harper's estate owed an extra $330,000.

Therefore, if you're going to transfer assets to an FLP (or an LLC), to reduce gift and estate tax, act in a businesslike manner. Document all transfers into the FLP and treat the FLP as a legal entity. Keep management power from the limited partners and don't commingle FLP funds with your own.

Ideally, you should have a non-tax reason for setting up an LLC, such as consolidating assets or introducing younger family members to the responsibility of managing those assets. Such reasons should be mentioned in the partnership agreement and subsequent actions should show you attempted to achieve those goals.

CLOSE CALLS

Among the assets that you might want to give away, you should consider shares in a closely held company that you own. Often, such shares will make up a substantial part of your estate. If you hold onto your shares until you die, you may stick your children with a huge tax bill. They might wind up having to sell the company to an outsider, just to pay the tax bill.

Giving away shares isn't always ideal, though. You may be relying upon a sale of the company to provide you with retirement income. Therefore, you may want to consider sophisticated techniques for selling your company to your kids, rather than giving it to them. If you are ready to pass your company to your kids, in return for a stream of retirement income, consider the following techniques:

- Installment Sale. You can sell your company to your children on an installment basis. Terms may be worked out so the payments are manageable; interest must be charged on the deferred payments, based on rates published monthly by the IRS.

  Such a sale will trigger capital gains unless the sale is made to an income tax defective trust. (See Chapter 5 for further discussion.) If you have a low basis in your shares, but capital gains tax rates (15%) are lower than the gift and estate tax rates facing your family (up to 48% in 2004), using an installment sale permits the deferral of capital gains tax over the life of the arrangement yet the sale removes not only the shares but also any future appreciation from your estate.

- Private Annuity. Here, you transfer your shares to your successor, who agrees to pay you over your life expectancy. Suppose you're 55 years old, with a company valued at $5 million. You're ready to retire and have your daughter run the business.

  Actuarially, you have a 28-year life expectancy. Depending on current interest rates, your daughter might agree to pay you about $500,000 per year. (If she pays less, gift tax would be triggered.) Part of each payment would be a tax-free return of principal, part would be a tax-favored long-term gain, and part would be ordinary income.

  Where is the tax advantage? At your death, the annuity obligation ends. Even if your daughter has made only a few payments, no further payments are necessary. And no gift or estate tax will be triggered.

  Thus, if your daughter makes only three payments she will have acquired a $5 million company for only $1.5

million–and you will have removed a $5 million asset from your taxable estate without incurring a taxable gift.

Therefore, private annuities work best if the seller is in relatively poor health and unlikely to reach his life expectancy. However, deathbed transfers won't work: there must be at least a 50% chance the seller will live another year for a private annuity to pass muster.

- Self-Canceling Installment Notes (SCINs). The major risk with a private annuity is that the seller will live "too long." If you have a 28-year life expectancy but live for another 40 years, your daughter will have to keep coming up with $500,000, year after year.

  SCINs solve this problem. That's because the obligation to make payments have a fixed term. After a certain number of years, no further payments are due.

  However, if the seller dies before the term of the note, the obligation dies, too. The company belongs to the buyer, with no gift or estate tax consequences. (The seller's estate may recognize unreported gain, though.)

  In order for SCINs to work, the buyer must pay some premium for this cancellation feature. Generally, that means paying an above-market interest rate so that each annual payment is a bit higher than it would be, in a straight installment sale.

  Again, SCINs are most appropriate if the seller has a life expectancy less than the amount on the official actuarial tables.

AN ESOP IS NO FABLE

Yet another strategy is to sell your closely held company to an ESOP (employee stock ownership plans) rather than to your children. ESOPs are favored by the tax code, in order to encourage employee ownership of the company for which they work. Among the major tax advantages: if you sell all or part of your company to an ESOP, you can avoid paying taxes on your capital gains.

To enjoy this break, the ESOP must own at least 30% of the company. If so, you can avoid paying capital gains taxes by reinvesting the proceeds within 12 months in "qualified replacement property" (QRP), which can be any stock or bond issued by a U.S. operating company. While you retain ownership of your QRP, you'll never have to pay tax on the gain.

Say your basis in your company is $100,000 and you sell the entire company to an ESOP for $5 million, the fair market value. Ordinarily, you'd have a $4.9 million taxable gain and owe $980,000 to the IRS, at a 20% rate.

Instead, you can use the $5 million in sales proceeds to buy QRP. While you hold onto those domestic stocks and bonds, you avoid paying the $980,000 tax bill.

Under current law, if you hold those securities until death, the QRP will be treated as appreciated property, so your heirs will inherit with a step-up in basis and the deferred capital gain will disappear.

It is true that the 2001 tax law would reduce this basis step-up and might lead to a tax on inherited assets such as QRP in some situations, starting with deaths occurring in 2010. However, it is by no means certain that this provision actually will become effective.

Another, more pressing problem may arise. You may want to sell the securities you have acquired as QRP. Or, if you have purchased bonds to provide retirement income, those bonds may mature or be called prematurely. Once you no longer own the QRP you acquired, the deferred tax will be triggered–$980,000 in the above example, if all the QRP is sold—as well as tax on any subsequent appreciation. No rollovers are allowed.

To address this concern, major financial institutions offer ESOP notes to investors. ESOP notes are publicly registered securities, issued by highly rated companies such as Ford Motor Credit, ITT

Financial, Xerox Credit Corporation, and General Electric Capital Corporation. ESOP notes typically mature in 60 years, with 30-year call protection. They carry floating-rate coupons, indexed to 30-day commercial paper.

Fortunately, you're not locked into these fixed-income securities for 60 years. Generally, ESOP notes can be margined up to 75%-80% of their market value. That is, you can borrow against the face value of the notes and invest elsewhere, for growth as well as income.

Borrowers typically pay interest that's a shade higher than the broker call rate (3%, in late 2002). That expense is largely offset by the income earned on the ESOP notes. What's more, the interest you pay on such loans may be deductible, assuming you have sufficient investment income. Thus, for a modest cost, you can access a substantial portion of your initial sale proceeds without triggering any tax liability.

Suppose, for example, you sell your company for $5 million, as described above. You can use the $5 million to buy ESOP notes from your broker. Then you can borrow as much as $4 million against the notes and invest that money however you prefer, without triggering a capital gain. If you die before the ESOP notes mature or are called, your heirs may avoid ever paying tax on your lifetime capital gains.

A MATTER OF PRINCIPAL

If the ESOP borrows the money used to finance the stock purchase, your company could effectively re-pay the loan, by making contributions to the ESOP. When the company re-pays the loan in this manner, it can deduct principal as well as the interest payments. As a result, the total tax savings, to you and to the company, may be as great as two-thirds of the purchase price. Moreover, control of the company may remain with a successor you have designated, as owner (of shares not held by the ESOP) or manager.

In order to qualify for the above tax advantages, these conditions must be met:

- The selling shareholder must be an individual, a trust, an estate, a partnership, or an S corporation. The seller must have owned the stock sold to the ESOP for at least three years.
- The selling shareholder must not have received the stock from a qualified retirement plan (such as an ESOP or stock bonus plan), by exercising a stock option, or via an employee stock purchase program.
- The stock sold to the ESOP must be voting common stock (or preferred stock that is convertible into voting common stock).
- The company's stock cannot have been publicly traded for the 12 months preceding the sale to the ESOP.
- After the sale, the ESOP must own at least 30% of the company stock.
- The selling shareholder must reinvest the sale proceeds in QRP within 12 months after the sale. (An investment within the preceding three months also will qualify.)
- For certain periods, the stock purchased by the ESOP may not be allocated to the seller, the seller's relatives, or anyone who owns more than 25% of the company's remaining stock.
- The company establishing the ESOP must be a C corporation (not an S corporation). Although S corporations are now allowed to have ESOPs, thanks to recent tax law changes, their owners aren't eligible for the lifetime tax deferral.

You might, though, run your company as a regular C corporation until you sell the required number of shares to the ESOP, in order to qualify for the deferral. Then the company can elect S corporation status, to get S corporation benefits, such as relief from the corporate income tax. If your C corporation has no ESOP it could create one. You could sell stock to the ESOP and then have the company elect S corporation status.

As long as the above conditions are met, you can take advantage of this unique tax deferral. What's more, you can keep control of your company, if desired, because the ESOP only has to own 30% of the stock.

Thus, if you're the sole owner of a closely held corporation with no one to buy your stock, an ESOP can buy your entire company from you. Alternatively, you might sell at least 30% of your company to an ESOP and use the proceeds to diversify, without having to pay capital gains tax, as explained above. As long as you retain more than 50% of the shares, you retain control.

Moreover, an ESOP may be valuable even if you're not a sole owner. Say you have a 50-50 co-owner who is unwilling or unable to buy your shares. As another option, you could sell your holdings to an ESOP and defer paying taxes on capital gains, perhaps forever.

BUILDING A BETTER BUY-SELL

If your company has one or more co-owners, you should have a buy-sell agreement to protect yourself and your family.

- Protecting yourself. If you retire or become disabled, someone will be obliged to buy you out, providing you with needed income.
- Protecting your family. If you die while still running the business, a buy-sell can guarantee that someone will adequately reimburse your heirs.

There's another aspect to a buy-sell agreement: the buy side. If one of your co-owners retires, dies, becomes disabled, or simply leaves the company, a buy-sell can allow you to retain control of the company. You won't have unwanted replacements for the outgoing owner.

A buy-sell agreement may have tax benefits, too. A contract negotiated between you and unrelated co-owners provides a valuation you can rely upon for gift and estate tax purposes as long as it's a bona fide, arm's-length agreement.

How do you go about putting together a buy-sell that will accomplish all of these goals?

- Your buy-sell should be a formal written agreement.
- It should specifically identify the seller, the buyer, the trigger events (retirement death, disability, etc.), and the terms of the sale.
- The agreement should include a price for transaction and a mechanism for keeping the price current.

Suppose, for example, your company has four unrelated equal co-owners. You agree the company is now worth $5 million, so each owner's interest is valued at $1.25 million.

Under the terms of the buy-sell, you might meet every January to formally renegotiate a new value for the calendar year. Another approach is to use a formula: you might state that your company is worth a certain multiple of book value or net operating income.

Whatever you do, don't wait to set a valuation. When you are ready to retire, for example, you'll lack leverage to negotiate with your co-owners or successors.

You should enter into a buy-sell agreement as soon as possible. If you and your co-owners keep putting it off, the addition of new partners may serve as a catalyst.

There are two ways to structure a buy-sell:

1. <u>Cross-purchase.</u> The successor or the remaining principals are required to buy the ownership interest from a departing owner. The new owners get a basis step-up when they buy the interest, which is likely to reduce the tax owed on a subsequent sale. Moreover, if a cross-purchase buy-sell is funded with life insurance there is no exposure to the alternative minimum tax (AMT) or to an IRS charge of constructive dividends.
2. <u>Redemption.</u> The company buys in the shares of the departing owner. The remaining owners keep their interests, but

their proportionate interest in the business is increased as the other interests are retired.

Because of the basis step-up, most buy-sells are structured as cross-purchase agreements, with each owner required to buy the ownership interest of a deceased, retiring, disabled, or withdrawing owner. However, if a number of buyers are involved, a redemption agreement is sometimes used to simplify the purchase.

If you want to keep your business in the family, your buy-sell will be between yourself and a family member. To prevent a challenge from the IRS, have an independent appraiser value the company.

Moreover, if a redemption agreement is used, make certain that no family member who is also a beneficiary of the estate owns or will own stock. Otherwise, the redemption price would be treated as a taxable dividend. A better alternative: have the family member purchase the stock from the estate.

ENSURING A SUCCESSION PLAN

Funding is important, too: how will the buyer manage to pay for the seller's interest in the company? A moderately successful business might be worth $5 million these days. If there are four equal co-owners, the death of one might generate a $1.25 million buyout obligation. Neither the surviving owners nor the company may have enough cash for the buyout.

Often, buy-sell agreements are funded by life insurance. Each shareholder holds a policy on the other's life. That will provide the buyout cash in case of death.

Suppose you have three co-owners and you want a cross-purchase buy-sell. Rather than have four people each own three insurance policies, one policy may be purchased on each owner, to be held in escrow or in trust. (If a cross-purchase buy-sell is used, be sure that life insurance premiums are paid by the individuals and not by the corporation. If the company pays the premiums, such payments may be re-cast as taxable compensation or dividends.)

In addition, if each shareholder purchases an insurance policy on the lives of each shareholder, the decedent owner's survivors may wind up on the short end of the stick. Suppose there are four equal co-owners of a $5 million company. Al dies so Bonnie, Carl, and Dave collect the insurance proceeds and pay Al's estate $1.25 million for his share. Now Al's heirs have $1.25 million but the other three owners have a $5 million company (worth $1.67 million per owner), even though Al paid as much for the insurance as his three co-owners.

To deal with the problem of disproportionate results, the insurance policy might have a higher death benefit: 50% of the company's value if there are three owners, 33% with four owners, etc. Thus, such a strategy will be more expensive than buying a collection of individual policies.

If Al dies, the policy will pay $1.67 million. The buy-sell would call for 25% of the proceeds (about $417,000) to go to each of the owners, including Al's estate. After the buyout, then, Art's estate would wind up with $1.67 million, the same as the value of the shares owned by the surviving shareholders.

If the policy is held in a trust, estate tax can be avoided. In addition, your company may want to arrange for disability buy-out insurance, to fund a buy-sell that takes effect because an owner no longer can work.

What about buyouts triggered by retirement or just leaving the company? Typically, such buyouts are paid over several years. A cap may be placed on the annual payout to allow the company to stay in business without borrowing excessively to pay a former owner.

Chapter 5
A Thorough Look At Trusts

Although some types of trusts can help you save taxes, including estate taxes, that's not their only purpose–or even their main purpose. In essence, a trust is an entity created to hold the title to certain assets.

Every trust must have a trustee, who'll manage the trust assets, and a beneficiary or beneficiaries. Beyond those generalities, trusts can be divided into two categories:

<u>Revocable trusts.</u> As the name suggests, these trusts can be materially changed or canceled altogether. A revocable trust must be created during your lifetime, rather than at your death. When you hear or read about "living" trusts, those are usually references to revocable trusts.

You generally can serve as trustee and beneficiary of a revocable trust you create. Therefore, you can retain control over any assets you transfer into the trust. If you become ill or incompetent, a successor trustee can take over management of the trust assets. There will be no costly, public, time-consuming court battle over control of your finances.

Michael Walker, for example, had no spouse or children so his estate was to go to his two nieces. As he grew older, he no longer could care for himself. Michael's nieces, then, could have used his assets to provide him with quality long-term care...or they might not, hoping to preserve their inheritance.

Fortunately, Michael had drawn up a revocable trust, naming a local bank along with the nieces as successor trustees. The trust documents called for the successors to provide him with the best possible care and the bank made sure this instruction was carried out.

As an additional benefit, assets held in a revocable trust avoid the time and expense of going through probate. In many states, probate is not that burdensome or expensive. However, if you own property in another state, your survivors will have to go through a separate probate for the out-of-state asset. That may mean hiring an attorney, long-distance, or making unwanted trips. Holding out-of-state property in a revocable trust avoids this "ancillary" probate as well as local probate.

BARE FACTS

While using a revocable trust to hold out-of-state property may work well for a vacation home, such trusts may not be appropriate for investment property. Some people put investment property into a revocable living trust to avoid probate–then they get sued because a child swallowed some paint containing lead and they have to pay huge amounts. If the property is held inside a Limited Liability Company (LLC) or a Family Limited Partnership (FLP) instead, your personal assets may be protected.

Therefore, revocable trusts won't provide any asset protection. Assets held in a revocable trust are just as vulnerable to your creditors as assets you hold personally. Moreover, there are no tax benefits to setting up a revocable trust: the income will be taxed to you and the trust assets will be included in your taxable estate.

WINNING THE TITLE GAME

However, there are intangible benefits to creating a revocable trust, such as the need to get your affairs in order. This will help you manage your property as you grow older and assist your heirs in handling your estate.

For example, Nancy Thomas created a revocable trust and began the process of re-titling her assets to the trust. She discovered she had 17 mutual funds, four brokerage accounts, and two bank accounts. In re-titling her assets, Nancy consolidated them to a few accounts so record keeping was easier while expenses were reduced.

PASSING LANE

What will happen to the assets in your living trust after your death? No matter how rich or powerful you are, you can't take those assets with you. It didn't work for the Pharaohs of ancient Egypt, who built the Great Pyramids to hold their jewels and horses and dogs, and it won't work for you.

Instead, the assets in your living trust will be distributed according to the language of the trust. When your draw up your living trust you'll provide for the disposition of those assets after your death.

If you wish, you can have the assets in your living trust go directly to your spouse, your children, and other heirs. Such an estate plan may be dangerous, though.

If your assets are passed outright to heirs, they will be exposed to all types of creditors, including divorcing spouses and bankruptcy courts. Considering how the legal system in this country is constantly finding new "rights" for plaintiffs, who knows whether your heirs will be sued, on outrageous grounds, and wind up having to pay a sizable award for damages?

Besides, your heirs may be subject to failing health or just poor judgment. The assets you worked hard to accumulate might wind up in the hands of some con artist.

To prevent such calamities, you can provide that the assets of your living trust will pour-over into an irrevocable trust at your death. Such a trust can be a dynasty trust, meant to support your heirs and even your yet-unborn descendants for years to come.

Irrevocable trusts. If you want asset protection or tax savings you'll have to create an irrevocable trust to hold your assets. Such trusts can't be rescinded after they go into effect, which might be during your lifetime or after your death.

Income generated by an irrevocable trust may be taxable to the trust rather than to any individual. However, trust tax rates are higher than individual tax rates so it's common to invest trust assets in tax-efficient vehicles, such as low-dividend growth stocks.

Estate tax savings may be realized, though. Once assets are out of your possession, in an irrevocable trust, they're out of your taxable estate, too, and the same goes for any future appreciation.

If you transfer, say, $500,000 to an irrevocable trust and invest that money in growth stocks, the trust fund might eventually expand to $2 million, $5 million, or more without being subject to estate taxes.

Moreover, creating an irrevocable trust offers additional advantages. As is the case with revocable trusts, assets in an irrevocable trust won't go through probate and won't get tangled up in messy incompetency hearings. They offer creditor protection, too, if the trust is properly drafted. As a result, the trust assets may be safe if you wind up on the losing end of a lawsuit.

Assets held in trust may be kept safely for loved ones, too. You might be concerned, for example, that your surviving spouse won't be able to preserve inherited wealth; that a disabled heir will have special needs; or that one of your children may be tempted to spend money unwisely. All of these issues can be addressed by transferring your assets to an irrevocable trust, as long as the language of the trust documents express your intentions and the trustee is careful with the trust fund.

Assets held inside an irrevocable trust may also be protected from marital property settlements. If your son or daughter is involved in a divorce, those assets may not be subject to any division because they won't actually belong to your child. Nevertheless, the trustee may be authorized to provide your son or daughter with cash for a down payment on a home perhaps, or money to start a business.

TAPPING THE RIGHT TRUSTEE

As you can see, one key to using a trust is to find a trustee who'll be both prudent and cooperative, after your death. Not every trustee lives up to the ideal, though.

For example, Paul Sawyer was the beneficiary of a trust that entitled him to the trust's income plus access to principal for "health, education, maintenance, and welfare" needs. For 10 years, Paul didn't ask for a distribution from principal. Then, when he requested funds for his health care–which was clearly allowed by the trust language–the bank serving as trustee refused.

Another case involved Rose Peterson, 80 years old, a trust beneficiary who fell in a shopping mall and broke her eyeglasses. She needed $300 for a new pair so she asked the trustee. The trustee, another bank officer, said that would be okay but the trust committee just met and another meeting wasn't scheduled until a month later.

How can you prevent such future disasters, especially after you're not around to exert any influence? Most recently created trusts provide for trustee replacement. That is, a majority of the beneficiaries can vote to replace one corporate trustee with another. If you draw up a trust in order to protect your loved ones in the unforeseeable future, you probably should put some language in the trust documents permitting them to jettison a troublesome trustee.

ACCORDING TO PLAN

One increasingly popular use of irrevocable trusts is to name such a trust as beneficiary of your IRA.

If you're reluctant to name an individual as beneficiary of your IRA, you can name a trust as IRA beneficiary and also name the intended recipients as trust beneficiaries. Then the trustee can take money from the IRA and pass it through to the trust beneficiaries. In certain cases, such a plan makes sense: rather than name a minor or an incompetent person or a spendthrift as IRA beneficiary, you'd rather rely upon a responsible trustee.

However, the IRS issued final regulations on required distributions in 2002 and it's possible that the trust you already have named as IRA beneficiary won't conform to the new regulations. As a result, your heirs may not enjoy maximum tax deferral, which can cost them a great deal of total wealth.

To achieve maximum tax deferral with a trust as IRA beneficiary, four elements must be in place:

- The trust must be valid under state law.
- The trust must be irrevocable. (You can use a revocable trust that becomes irrevocable after your death.)
- The individual trust beneficiaries must be clearly identifiable.
- Trust documents must be provided to the IRA custodian.

If all four conditions are met, the IRA may be distributed over the life expectancy of the trust beneficiary. Suppose, for example, Greg Jones leaves his IRA to a trust and names his daughter Susan as trust beneficiary. After Greg's death, Susan has a 21-year life expectancy so the IRA may be stretched out over 21 years, extending tax-deferred accumulation.

CAUGHT IN THE CONTINGENCY

The new regulations, however, may make it difficult to achieve such a desirable result with a trust as IRA beneficiary. In many cases, the IRS will insist that all but remote contingent beneficiaries will be considered for the purpose of determining a payout after your death. This may include some contingent or remainder beneficiaries.

Suppose Greg not only named a trust as IRA beneficiary and his daughter as trust beneficiary. He also named his grandchildren as contingent trust beneficiaries while a charity was named to receive the remainder of what's in the trust, after the death of all these beneficiaries.

If the trust does not contain the right language the IRA may have to be distributed over the shortest life expectancy among all the beneficiaries. In this example, it likely would be the charity, which has no life expectancy, so the IRA would fall under a five-year rule, requiring complete distribution within five years.

GO WITH THE CASH FLOW

Fortunately, such results can be avoided with shrewd planning. One tactic is to make sure a trust you name as IRA beneficiary is a conduit trust. Such a trust might require that 100% of the IRA minimum distribution is immediately paid out to the trust beneficiaries.

That is, after your death minimum distributions must be made from an inherited IRA. If you leave a $1 million IRA and the first-year required distribution is 4%, then at least $40,000 must be withdrawn (and made subject to income tax) that year. If this $40,000 must be paid out immediately to the trust beneficiaries, the trust will be treated as a conduit and secondary beneficiaries won't be considered for purposes of calculating life expectancy.

CUMULATIVE EFFECT

In some cases, though, you might not want to have all the money paid out from the trust to the trust beneficiary. Instead, you'd prefer to give the trustee discretion over paying out money to the trust beneficiaries. This approach can reduce the opportunity for long-term tax deferral, though.

To see how problems might arise, consider a 2002 Private Letter ruling from the IRS. In this situation, a grandmother named a trust as IRA beneficiary and named her two minor grandchildren as primary beneficiaries of the trust. Contingent beneficiaries were named, including the grandchildren's aunt, who was 67 years old in the year following the IRA owner's death.

Normally, required distributions would be based on the life expectancy of the oldest primary beneficiary—the older grandchild's life expectancy would be used. However, in this case the trustee had the discretion to make distributions for the grandchildren's support, health, and maintenance until they reached 30. After that age, each beneficiary could withdraw their entire share of the IRA.

The contingent beneficiaries were to inherit if both grandchildren died before reaching age 30. Ordinarily, this would not be a problem. In this case, though, the trustee had the discretion on whether or not to make distributions to the beneficiaries. The IRS called this a "contingency over and above the death of a prior beneficiary." The language of the trust, therefore, did not require that the payments from the IRA be paid out to the grandchildren each year. It was possible that unpaid IRA distributions would be accumulated in the trust.

As a result, the contingent beneficiaries had to be included among all the beneficiaries, for the purpose of determining which one had the shortest life expectancy. So the IRA had to be drawn down over the life expectancy of the 67-year-old aunt rather than the much longer life expectancy of the older grandchild.

DISTRIBUTION DIRECTIVES

Considering this ruling, if your estate plan calls for the use of a trust as IRA beneficiary, you probably should follow these guidelines:

- The Trustee should be required to pay out the required distributions to the primary beneficiaries. While these trust beneficiaries are minors, distributions can be made to custodial accounts. If this requirement is in place, the trustee may be given discretion to pay out additional money for the trust beneficiaries' health, education, support or maintenance.
- If older contingent beneficiaries are named, they should become beneficiaries only upon the death of the primary beneficiary.

With such an approach, IRA distributions can be stretched over the life expectancy of the oldest primary beneficiary.

GOING SEPARATE WAYS

An even better result might occur if multiple trust beneficiaries are named. Generally, distributions must be stretched over the age of the oldest beneficiary. If Greg Jones, in the previous example, had named his daughter Joan and his son Paul, along with Susan as trust beneficiaries, after his death Joan–the oldest–has a 17-year life expectancy so the IRA must be paid out over 17 years.

In some circumstances, each of the children may be able to take distributions over his or her own life expectancy. The final regulations allow multiple IRA beneficiaries to extend tax-deferral over their own life expectancies. If you name three children as IRA beneficiaries, each may be able to use his or her own life expectancy to withdraw the appropriate portion of the inherited IRA.

To achieve this result, separate shares must be created in the beneficiary designation form for the IRA. If so, by September 30th of the year following the year of the IRA owner's death, each beneficiary must establish a separate account and use his or her individual life expectancy for a withdrawal rate.

A similar result could occur in the above example, where Greg has named a trust as IRA beneficiary, with Joan, Susan, and Paul as trust beneficiaries. Separate accounts must be established in the IRA owner's designated beneficiary form and the trust document.

Again, separate accounts should be established by September 30th of the year following the year of the IRA owner's death. This would allow the three trust beneficiaries to stretch out distributions over their own life expectancy, to the benefit of the younger beneficiaries.

Whether or not the above strategy is adopted, naming an estate as a trust beneficiary can be a huge mistake. Suppose that trust assets are to be payable to a beneficiary's estate if that beneficiary dies before reaching a certain age. Now the estate is among the beneficiaries and an estate, like a charity, has no life expectancy.

In such a situation, if the IRA owner dies before the date he must begin to take minimum distributions, the IRA will have to be paid out within five years. If the owner dies after that date, distributions can be taken over his remaining life expectancy. In neither case can the distributions be stretched out over the beneficiary's life expectancy and there may be a substantial loss of tax-deferred growth. Therefore, you probably should avoid naming an estate as a backup beneficiary.

These pitfalls must be considered if you want to name a trust as IRA beneficiary. Chances are, if an IRA trust already is in your estate plan, it doesn't contain the language necessary for assuring a long stretch out. In that case, you might want to change your IRA beneficiary designation, naming a newly created trust designed to comply with the new regulations. Work with a knowledgeable professional who has extensive experience in this intricate area of the tax law.

LIFE AFTER TAX REFORM

Another popular use of irrevocable trusts is to hold a life insurance policy. That was the case for John Clark and his wife Joanne, who did their estate planning in 1999, when they expected to accumulate a $3 million estate. Their financial advisor anticipated they would both die after 2005, when each spouse could pass on $1 million worth of assets to their children, leaving an estimated $1 million subject to estate tax.

Assuming that taxes and other immediate expenses would come to around $500,000, the advisor recommended they buy a $500,000, second-to-die insurance policy, held in an irrevocable trust, to provide liquidity so the estate assets could remain intact. Since then, the Clarks have paid thousands of dollars a year in premiums.

In 2003, the picture seems a bit different. The Clarks' investments and stock options aren't worth as much as they were a few years ago so the assets in their estates might not total $3 million. In the current economic climate, the Clarks would prefer to retain those thousands of dollars spent on life insurance every year.

Perhaps most important, the 2001 tax law reduced the likely impact of future estate taxes for a short period. The per-person exemption already has moved up to $1 million, with a further increase to $1.5 million scheduled for deaths occurring in 2004. By 2009, that effective exemption amount will be $3.5 million. Barring additional legislation, the federal estate tax is scheduled to disappear in 2010 and reappear in 2011, with a $1 million exemption. If the Clarks wind up with no estate tax bill at all, why should they keep paying the premiums for this policy? If the internal rate of return, money in versus death benefit payable to heirs is a good investment, and premiums can be paid without compromising the Clark's lifestyle.

GUESSING GAME

An educated guess on the future of estate taxation may be necessary to answer that question. Many advisors doubt that the estate tax will be repealed. By the time we come to the date for scheduled repeal, there will be much greater demands on the Social Security system. An increasing number of people are likely to be dying then, with sizable estates, and the federal government probably will want the revenue.

If the estate tax isn't repealed, the size of the exemption amount will become the key issue. Many people who would have estate tax concerns with a $1 million exemption amount wouldn't be affected if each person could pass on $2 million or $3.5 million, tax-free. It is likely that some of the scheduled increases in the exemption will remain, even if the estate tax is not entirely repealed.

If the estate tax stays in place, with a higher exemption level, as many people expect, people with estates in the $1.5 million to $3.5 million range ($3 million to $7 million for married couples) might not face estate tax. What should such people do? That depends on your individual circumstances. Those who are only marginally in estate tax situations may not need their insurance any longer–if you expect your estate to be worth, say, $2 million, you might think about winding down insurance policies bought primarily to pay estate taxes.

This "winding down" might be done apace with the tax law. That is, your planning should be based on the idea that you could die at any time, no matter how healthy you are. A married couple might plan on being able to shelter up to $2 million worth of assets in 2003. If your estate is larger, life insurance may be needed to pay the estate tax bill. In 2004 (assuming no further changes in the interim), the amount that you can pass on, tax-free, goes up to $3 million, and insurance might be adjusted accordingly. Similar moves could be taken in the future, as the estate exemption increases.

BEYOND DEATH AND TAXES

Even if money isn't needed for estate tax, there still may be situations where life insurance should be retained. You might, for example, use insurance to equalize inheritances, if a business is being left to one child. Another use of life insurance might be to make a large charitable bequest without depleting the assets left to your heirs. Retaining a policy may be advisable if you have a health condition that has shortened your life expectancy.

In some cases, though, insurance policies already in place might be deemed unnecessary. If so, what can be done with those existing policies? One option is to enter into a 1035 exchange (named after a section of the tax code), tax-free, for a deferred annuity. Then you can either stop paying the insurance premiums or pay a smaller amount. The new contract eventually might be annuitized, providing a partially tax-sheltered stream of income.

Remember, if an insurance policy that was acquired for estate tax liquidity is held inside an irrevocable life insurance trust—which frequently will be the case—it's up to the trustee to make the 1035 exchange.

Another option is to simply stop paying the premiums on a policy held in trust, letting it lapse, but another solution might be preferable. That is, it probably would be better for the trustee to surrender the policy. The cash received for the policy can be kept in the trust, if desired.

You also should be aware that this life insurance decision does not have to be between surrendering the policy and paying the premiums in full. Although you can't increase coverage without a physical exam, you can decrease coverage. You might want to keep an existing policy in place while the exemption amount is $1.5 million, for example. As the exemption increases to $2 million and $2.5 million, the insurance coverage might be reduced, resulting in lower premiums.

A CHANGE IN PLAN

Indeed, Harry Richardson is currently scaling back a policy he bought a few years ago. At the time, Harry and his wife Teri purchased a $3.5 million, second-to-die policy to be held in trust. This policy would pay at the death of the second spouse, when the children would inherit and owe estate taxes.

Harry and Teri expected to have a sizable estate and to owe a considerable amount in tax. Moreover, one of their largest assets is a piece of real estate meant to be a family compound: a place where their three children could get together regularly, through the years. The insurance was to provide liquidity so the property would not have to be sold to pay estate tax.

Things look different to Harry and Teri now. Their estate tax liability may not be as great, under the revised tax law; the property, in a resort area, has lost value in the recession. Perhaps most important, their three grown children, who are scattered across the country, haven't shown much interest in going to retreats at this family compound. So the couple probably will sell this property, converting an illiquid asset to cash, which reduces their need for life insurance.

At the same time, Harry and Teri are not eager to keep paying the $30,000 annual premium. Paying the premiums will help their children in the future by providing a larger inheritance, but the couple would prefer to give money to their children now to help with immediate needs.

What will they do? One strategy is to stop paying premiums. They will be able to keep a much smaller death benefit–say, $750,000 or $1 million–in place for a number of years. That's because they have some equity in the policy and the annual mortality costs on a second-to-die policy are relatively low.

Another option would be to pay a lower premium for a policy with a face value somewhere between $1 million and $3.5 million. Alternatively, the trustee could just surrender the policy.

With any of these strategies, though, some surrender charges are likely to be due. If dropping a $3.5 million policy would trigger a $15,000 surrender charge, for example, reducing the face value by one-half might result in a $7,500 surrender charge.

WELL-DONE BUT RARE

Although reducing life insurance that was purchased to pay estate tax may make sense, such cutbacks tend to be rare. Most policies bought for estate liquidity are being retained, at least for now. Permanent life insurance typically has surrender penalties during the first 10 to 15 years. Therefore, many people who own permanent life policies are maintaining them until the uncertainty surrounding estate tax law is settled.

Moreover, if you want to increase your insurance–add new insurance to an existing estate plan–you may want to buy 10-year, level-premium term insurance or a Universal Life policy designed more like a term policy. The same is true if you are developing a new plan.

With the uncertainty surrounding the tax law, you can hedge your bets. Instead of buying permanent insurance, buy level-premium term insurance that is convertible to cash-value life during the full 10-year term. By buying convertible term, you minimize your cash outlay while maintaining the option to convert to permanent insurance without evidence of insurability.

Some insurers are offering second-to-die convertible term, as well as permanent insurance with a no-surrender-charge "bailout" clause that will take effect if specified down-with-estate-tax legislation is passed.

In the meantime, life insurance is still being bought to fund estate tax obligations. In some cases, second-to-die variable Universal Life policies are being used to fund "spousal lifetime access" trusts. As the name suggests, one spouse funds such a trust while the other spouse has access to the trust assets, which can in turn be used for the grantor's support, if necessary.

You also should evaluate other opportunities that may be available. Senior life settlement companies buy used life insurance contracts. These deals involve the purchase of a viable life insurance policy by a third party who'll keep the policy in force and eventually collect the proceeds. By selling, you may be able to unlock the profits you've accumulated in an old life insurance policy.

Generally, policies are bought from individuals, aged 65 and up, who are not terminally ill but who are expected to die in less than 14 years. With cancer, heart attacks, diabetes, and so on, it's possible to get a fairly accurate idea of life expectancy. Often, buyers purchase a bundle of policies, spreading the longevity risk. Thus, pools of policies are turned into securities that are sold to investors who have interests in many policies. This approach minimizes the chance that a policy on your life will fall into hands of a single investor who then will have a huge incentive to expedite your demise.

A WEALTH OF ADVANTAGES

As indicated, an irrevocable trust used to hold life insurance may be part of a sophisticated estate plan. For an even more comprehensive plan, you can go beyond life insurance trusts to The Wealth Trust®.

The Wealth Trust®, a trademarked dynasty trust, can be coordinated with all the other elements of a sophisticated estate plan. These elements might include a Family Limited Partnership (FLP), Limited Liability Company (LLC), Charitable Remainder Trust (CRT), a Private Family Foundation, or any combination of the above. In addition, a thorough estate plan will encompass beneficiary designations for your IRA or other tax-advantaged retirement plan.

Regardless of your personal circumstances and the complexity of your estate plan, The Wealth Trust® can serve as the cornerstone for your family succession planning. The language of The Wealth Trust® can ensure that your loved ones live out their lives in comfort, with ample financial opportunities, while enjoying protection from severe reversals.

In particular, savvy estate lawyers can help you create The Wealth Trust® to receive the assets in your revocable living trust. Even if you don't create a revocable living trust, your will can direct that assets in your estate be transferred to The Wealth Trust®.

Here are some of the advantages The Wealth Trust® can offer:

- Creditor protection. Assets held in trust will not belong to any particular individual so they are not subject to lawsuits, divorce settlements, bankruptcy claims, and so on. No matter what happens to the tax code, assets held in The Wealth Trust® will still be protected from involuntary transfers.
- Tax shelter. Although the future of the federal estate tax is uncertain, most commentators feel that actual repeal is unlikely, given the federal government's commitments to increased military outlays as well as the projected future demands on Social Security and Medicare. More revenues will be required and it does not seem probable that a tax on "the rich" will be eliminated.

Moreover, a repeal of the federal estate tax would be the fourth such "abolition" of this tax. Each time it was abolished, an estate tax has been reintroduced, and that's likely to happen again.

Assuming that a federal estate tax continues to exist, assets held in The Wealth Trust® won't be included in anyone's estate and therefore won't be subject to estate tax. Careful planning can minimize or dispel the impact of the generation-skipping transfer tax.

- Access to capital. Even though assets held in The Wealth Trust® are beyond the reach of creditors and estate tax collectors, these assets are not forbidden to your loved ones, who can be named as trust beneficiaries. Trust assets can be distributed to those beneficiaries, as needed.

  When you create The Wealth Trust®, you'll name a trustee. This trustee will have a fiduciary responsibility to provide for the beneficiaries' well being, and to follow the instructions set forth by the trust creator.

  A capable trustee can provide trust funds in case of a medical emergency or an outstanding business opportunity. The trustee can help your descendants pay college bills, buy a starter home, pay for a glorious wedding, or take a-once-in-a-lifetime vacation.

  In essence, a trustee can act like a friendly banker, providing cash for life's truly important circumstances. Your loved ones and their loved ones won't be at the mercy of an impersonal bank, at a time when cash is crucial. All the while, the money left in trust can keep growing, undiminished by creditors' claims or foolish spending.

  What's more, if any trust beneficiary has special needs, such a trust is an ideal vehicle for providing the required care.

- Succession planning. Keeping assets in The Wealth Trust® provides a reasonable way to help your children grow into their inheritances. As described below, each of your children can eventually manage a Wealth Trust of his or her own.

Compared with an outright bequest of your entire estate, using The Wealth Trust® to transfer assets may be more prudent. Chances are it took you decades to build up a substantial net worth. If your children inherit too much, too soon, they may not appreciate what they have.

"Easy come" might result in "easy go," to your heirs' misfortune. On the other hand, assets held in The Wealth Trust® are subject to fiduciary responsibilities and are much more likely to be managed carefully.

- Future flexibility. The Wealth Trust® can be structured so that it eventually will divide into two or more trusts, perhaps one for each of your children. This ability can make The Wealth Trust® more manageable and less likely to create family friction.

LONG DIVISION

As mentioned, The Wealth Trust® is a variation of a dynasty trust, so it is meant to serve several generations. Some states even permit perpetual trusts, which may literally go on forever.

Obviously, there are advantages to putting assets in a trust where they can grow for many decades, sheltered from creditors and estate tax, yet still remain available to trust beneficiaries. However, over such a long time period, logistical problems may arise. A dynasty trust may eventually have dozens of beneficiaries, scattered around the world, with widely varying needs and capabilities. Even the most adept trustee may have trouble managing a trust under those circumstances.

Therefore, a sophisticated plan will call for the use of sub-trusts. You might, for example, create a Wealth Trust with your spouse, children, and grandchildren as beneficiaries.

You also can provide that The Wealth Trust® will divide into subtrusts after a certain number of years or after a certain event, such as the death of your spouse. If you have three children, The Wealth Trust® might be split into three sub-trusts, with equal assets.

It may be desirable to name each of your children as trustee of his or her own Wealth Trust. Provided the language of the trust is properly drafted, the trust assets won't be exposed to that child's creditors, or subject to estate tax.

At the death of each of your children, further division is possible, to sub-trusts for each of their children. And so on, as long as the trust remains in existence, with each sub-trust staying manageable in size yet able to provide for the beneficiaries, your descendants.

KEEP THE CASH FLOWING

As described above, The Wealth Trust® is capable of providing substantial benefits to your survivors. However, that assumes that The Wealth Trust® includes sufficient cash to handle obligations and opportunities as they arise.

The surest way to accomplish this goal is to include life insurance among the assets held in The Wealth Trust®. If The Wealth Trust® is created during your lifetime, and funded by life insurance, you can be certain the trust will hold a meaningful amount of cash at your death.

If you're married, you might want to fund The Wealth Trust®, at least in part, with less-expensive survivorship insurance that will pay off after the deaths of both spouses.

Why is it so important to have liquidity in The Wealth Trust®? Because a supply of ready cash can prevent an awkward or untimely liquidation of other assets.

Suppose, for example, that you have a sizable IRA and that your estate is large enough to generate an estate tax bill. If your heirs must tap the IRA to pay the estate tax bill, there will be an income tax bill as well and there may be little left in the IRA to grow tax-deferred for heirs.

On the other hand, suppose that The Wealth Trust® holds a life insurance policy, so that the proceeds are not subject to estate tax. With proper planning, the trustee can lend money to the estate to cover the estate tax obligation.

This will permit the full amount of the IRA to be stretched out, income tax deferred, over the beneficiaries' life expectancies. Recent legislative and regulatory developments make it likely that IRA balances will grow ever larger in the future; extending tax deferral can immensely increase the amounts that are passed on to your children and grandchildren.

What if the federal estate tax is repealed? As mentioned before, the estate tax probably will find its way back into law, before too long. Moreover, the repeal of the federal estate tax now is coupled with an introduction of a capital gains tax on appreciated estate assets, in some circumstances. Counting state capital gains tax, this might add up to a 25% tax.

In addition, federal estate tax repeal would cost many states their "sponge tax," a special type of estate tax that piggy-backs on the federal estate tax. To make up the shortfall, states may add estate taxes of their own, at rates that might reach 15%.

Future estate taxes may be assessed on an estate that is much larger than it is now. After an extended bear market, stocks are depressed, but they probably will rebound sharply in the coming years. You might expect a $3 million estate to become $4 million at the time of your death, a $6 million estate to become $8 million, and so on.

Beyond providing for taxes on a larger estate, good planning could call for an additional liquidity cushion of 10% or so, to help your heirs avoid selling high-quality assets at a bad time, just to raise cash. Considering all of the above factors, it's reasonable to desire a 50% cash reserve inside The Wealth Trust®, and life insurance remains the most cost-effective way of providing that needed cash.

Even without a future estate tax obligation, having life insurance in The Wealth Trust® can greatly enhance its advantages. Cash from life insurance proceeds can help divide estate assets among family members; such cash may provide the means of equalizing an estate when a family business is involved. In case of an unexpected need for cash or if a marvelous investment opportunity arises, there will be no need to sell assets in a rush, or at a market bottom.

SECOND HELPING

If The Wealth Trust® is a vital component of your estate planning, adding another Wealth Trust may be extremely helpful. Such a Wealth Trust may pay off via an innovative "Estate Freeze" strategy.

To see how this trust might work, consider George and Ellen Martin, who are in their mid-70s with four children and five grandchildren. Not only do they want to minimize estate taxes, they are extremely interested in privacy and keeping their holdings confidential.

George and Ellen established a second Wealth Trust that's purposely structured as a "defective" trust for income tax purposes. There are various methods for achieving this: here, George and Ellen retain the power to substitute other assets for those in this trust. This trust is also set up as a "grantor" trust: a trust where the grantor is responsible for the income taxes but the trust assets are out of the grantor's taxable estate.

This trust will be funded by a gift of $2 million worth of stocks and mutual funds. In effect, such a gift will use up a part of George and Ellen's $1 million estate tax shelters. No gift tax or estate tax will be due. The $2 million gift will also be allocated toward the $2 million+ exemption that George and Ellen have from the generation-skipping transfer tax.

The assets given to this trust will be outside George and Ellen's taxable estates, along with any future appreciation. However, as mentioned, this trust will be defective for income tax purposes. Thus, George and Ellen will pay the income tax on trust income. In effect, they can make additional gifts to their children and grandchildren (paying the income tax) without incurring a gift tax.

PARTNERSHIP PAYOFF

The next step in this Estate Freeze strategy calls for George and Ellen to establish the Martin Family Limited Partnership. Ellen and Greg would be the general partners, contributing $5 million worth of stocks, mutual funds and real estate. Initially, they would own the limited partnership interest as well.

The partnership agreement would restrict the rights of the limited partners so that the assets in the partnership will get a discount for gift and estate tax purposes. An independent appraiser might conclude that the lack of control and marketability reduces the $5 million worth of assets contributed by George and Ellen to a $3.5 million value.

In order for such a sale to be recognized, The Wealth Trust® must be a "trust of substance." As mentioned, George and Ellen have given $2 million to the trust, so it qualifies as a trust of substance.

Because The Wealth Trust® had substance, it was able to purchase the $5 million limited partnership interest. Moreover, because the general partner controls the limited partnership the assets were discounted by 30% resulting in a $3.5 million purchase price. Thus, for a $3.5 million note, The Wealth Trust® was able to purchase the limited partnership interest that held $5 million (face value) worth of assets. What's more, the $5 million note effectively held by George and Ellen is frozen: it will never increase in value even if the $5 million worth of assets in The Wealth Trust® appreciate.

Then the income-tax defective Wealth Trust could purchase the limited partnership interest for $3.5 million, paying with an interest-only installment note. The interest rate would be set at current levels, perhaps 4.5%.

Thus, The Wealth Trust® would be entitled to the income from $5 million worth of property, perhaps $300,000 per year. It will owe interest on the installment note: $175,000 at a 5% rate. The excess–$125,000 per year in this example–can be used to prepay the installment note, buy additional life insurance, or be distributed to the trust beneficiaries, their children. This is an excellent way to remove future appreciation from a taxable estate, in effect freezing the value for tax purposes.

Hence, the name Estate Freeze. When assets are transferred to The Wealth Trust® via an Estate Freeze, there is generally no tax on appreciation for multiple generations.

In some strategies, The Wealth Trust® will hold $3.5 million worth of life insurance on George and Ellen's lives. After George and Ellen die, the $3.5 million of life insurance will pay off the $3.5 million note.

If necessary, George as the general partner can sell off enough assets each year to pay the interest on the note, after paying capital gains tax. Because the trust is a grantor trust the income will be taxable to George and Ellen as a long-term capital gain, taxed at 20% or even 18% in the future. If the income had been taxable to the trust, the tax rate would be 35% or higher.

A FIRM FOUNDATION

At this point, George and Ellen may have removed most of the assets from their taxable estate. The rest of their assets can be left to their children but the George and Ellen Martin Family Foundation can be named as a contingent beneficiary.

Thus, their children can decide how much they wish to inherit and how much they wish to disclaim in favor of the family foundation. Assets passed to the family foundation will be sheltered from estate tax, so George and Ellen's estates might be untaxed with a full disclaimer.

Once the family foundation has been funded, at least 5% of the assets must be given to charity every year, so favorite causes can be supported. Family members may serve as officers and directors of this foundation, receiving compensation as well as having the responsibility for disbursing trust assets each year.

This Estate Freeze strategy is complicated so you need to work with a first-class estate planning attorney, if you're interested. The idea is to enable you to pass millions of dollars to your children and grandchildren, protected from future claimants and predators. Transfer taxes can be minimized, leaving more for your descendants and for qualified charitable organizations.

Chapter 6
Give And Take

As mentioned, trusts fall into two categories: revocable and irrevocable. Irrevocable trusts, moreover, may serve specialized purposes, such as life insurance trusts and dynasty trusts such as The Wealth Trust®.

Many other types of irrevocable trusts may be created, including some that are designed to benefit the grantor as well as the trust beneficiaries.

For example, with asset values and interest rates both down, this may be an ideal time to use a Grantor Retained Annuity Trust (GRAT). You can move substantial amounts from your taxable estate without owing a penny of gift tax.

Here's how a GRAT works. You transfer assets into an irrevocable trust. Pick a trust term you expect to outlive; if you die before the term ends, all of the assets go back into your taxable estate.

Then you select a payout that you'll receive from the trust each year. Because a GRAT is an annuity trust, you'll get a fixed amount: $50,000 per year, for example.

However, don't set the payout rate too high. If you take more income from the trust than you can use during your lifetime, you will wind up putting that unspent money back into your taxable estate and possibly paying estate taxes on it.

Upfront, you'll put a present value on your future income from the trust. That present value is subtracted from the amount you transfer to get the amount of the gift that eventually will go to the trust beneficiaries.

Say you transfer $1 million to a 15-year GRAT, with the trust assets going to your son Ed at the end of the term. If the present value of the income stream you'll receive is $900,000, you've made a $100,000 gift to Ed, which will have gift tax consequences. If the present value of your income stream is $950,000, you've made a $50,000 gift.

ZERO TOLERANCE

What's more, if the present value of your retained income is $1 million or more, you won't incur any gift tax at all. For years, the IRS insisted that you could not "zero out" a GRAT.

The Tax Court ruled otherwise in the Walton case (Audrey J. Walton v. Commissioner; 115 TC No. 41; No. 3824-99, December 22, 2000). In this case, Audrey (Sam Walton's widow) transferred $100 million worth of stock to a two-year GRAT. Under the terms of the trust, if she died within the two years, the payments would continue, to her estate.

The IRS put a value on the annuity payments and came up with a figure just over $96 million. Thus, Audrey was said to have made a taxable gift of nearly $4 million.

Audrey saw it another way. She put a value on the contingent interest (the chance the estate would receive annuity payments) and also subtracted this value from the gift, bringing the taxable gift down to a token $6,200. Now, zero-gift-tax GRATs are frequently drafted.

Currently, low interest rates make it easier to zero out a GRAT. That's because low interest rates raise the present value of the income you retain.

For example, in August 2002 the IRS discount rate was 5.2%. If you had set up a 15-year GRAT that would pay you $90,000 (9%) per year, your future income would be valued at $940,000 and you'd incur a $60,000 gift when you set it up.

Two months later, in October, that discount rate had fallen to 4.2%. The same income stream ($90,000 per year for 15 years) would be valued at $1 million so you'd owe no gift tax at all.

Thus, a period of low interest rates may be an ideal time to create a GRAT.

APPRECIATING LOW STOCK PRICES

In addition, today's low stock market values can make a GRAT an outstanding vehicle now. That's because a GRAT works best if the trust assets appreciate during the term.

Say you fund a GRAT with $1 million worth of depressed technology stocks. Such stocks don't pay dividends so you'll probably receive $90,000 per year in shares distributed from the trust.

If the stocks in the trust appreciate by 4.2%, the current discount rate, the result will be a wash and your heirs won't get anything from the GRAT. But if the stocks grow by more than 4.2% a year over 15 years (a likely scenario), the trust might wind up holding $100,000, $200,000, $500,000 or more in stocks.

No matter how much is left, your son Ed will get the entire trust fund–and not owe a penny in gift tax. All the assets passing to Ed, moreover, are out of your taxable estate.

If you don't want to fund a GRAT with depressed publicly traded shares, consider transferring shares of a closely held company to the trust. As long as the long-term appreciation tops the 4.2% discount rate, you can move a piece of the company out of your estate without triggering any gift tax.

Remember, though, that GRATs are irrevocable so you can't personally take the assets back later if you decide you need them. Be sure you can afford to lose control of those assets before placing them in the trust.

HOME RUNS

Another type of trust, a Qualified Personal Residence Trust (QPRT), can hold down the cost of keeping an expensive home in the family. Leaving your home to your kids can trigger an estate tax bill; giving them the house may generate a gift tax. Instead, give the house to a QPRT and name your children as the trust beneficiaries, for a huge tax saving.

QPRTs reduce gift tax and eliminate estate tax. You'll transfer a house (a principal residence or a vacation home) to a QPRT, retaining use of the house during the trust term. After the term of the trust, often five or 10 years, ownership of the house will pass to the trust beneficiaries, probably your children.

Therefore, you can use a QPRT to make a deferred gift. Because of this deferral, the value of the taxable gift is reduced. A house that's worth $600,000 might be removed from your estate yet the taxable gift might be valued at $300,000, $200,000, or even less.

The younger the donor, the longer the term, and the higher the level of prevailing interest rates, the smaller the taxable gift that will be incurred.

In most situations, QPRTs are structured so that the house will revert to your taxable estate if you die before the end of the trust term. This reversion feature provides the biggest discount, for gift tax purposes. The downside: if you die before the end of the trust term, the tax benefit will be lost.

Therefore, when you create a QPRT the term you designate is crucial. Generally, short terms work best for sick or elderly homeowners while younger donors can use longer terms.

If you're in good health, around age 70, a 10-year trust is often a good choice. At age 60, a 15-year trust may be a better option while a 20-year term may work well if you are 50 or younger. If longer terms are chosen, the added tax benefits probably won't be worth the extra risk of premature death.

When you consider a QPRT, there are several points to keep in mind:

- You can serve as the trustee, if desired. Thus, you'll remain in control of the house.
- You can establish two QPRTs as long as one is for a principal residence.
- QPRTs work best for transferring a debt-free house. If there still is a mortgage, ongoing payments will be considered additional contributions to the trust, which will confuse valuation.
- After the term ends, if you still want to live there you can rent it from the new owners (probably your children). This will move more money out of your estate, free of gift tax. The IRS has said that a prearranged leaseback is acceptable as long as the rent is fair.

GETTING PERSONAL

How far can you stretch the definition of "personal residence," to qualify for QPRT treatment? Pretty far, according to several IRS letter rulings (9841015, 9918042, 9918049, 9906014, 9916030).

- Acreage containing barns and sheds was allowed to be included in a QPRT, even though no commercial activity had been conducted on the property for years.
- Wooded property used as a large recreational area passed the test.
- A tennis cottage, caretaker's house, and adjacent land all qualified for low-taxed transfer via a QPRT.
- Rental property cannot qualify for QPRT treatment. However, the IRS has approved the QPRT tax break for a vacation home that included a separate rental apartment. Similarly, the rental of a caretaker house upon residential property didn't void the QPRT.

You may be reluctant to transfer a house to a QPRT for, say, 10 years if you have to turn over your home to your children then.

There's a way out, though: the QPRT documents can give you the option to lease the property from the new owners at the end of the trust term, at fair market value. The IRS has upheld this strategy in letter ruling 9918042.

The greater the actuarial chance of your dying during the QPRT term, the greater the tax deduction. Formerly, married couples could set these trusts up, using a wife rather than a husband as a donor, taking advantage of a unisex mortality table as well as an out-of-date mortality table.

Unfortunately, the IRS has issued more realistic mortality tables. Thus, QPRT creators can get the unisex tax break but not the mortality table break, so these trusts are slightly less appealing.

The new tables make a sizable difference for QPRTs established at age 80 or 85; a 10-year QPRT created by an 80-year-old client now results in a taxable gift that's 10.45% larger than under the old rules.

The impact upon younger grantors is much smaller: taxable gifts are increased by 3.20% and 2.34% for 65- and 60-year-old grantors, for example. Even with the new tables, though, a QPRT may be a tax-efficient way of removing a valuable home (complete with surrounding property) from your estate.

ON THE HOUSE

Unlike GRATs, QPRTs are adversely affected by falling interest rates: gift taxes are increased. Nevertheless, there are situations when a QPRT makes sense, even in a low-rate environment.

Steve Long, for example, was worth $10 million a few years ago. Now his net worth is around $7 million because of lower stock prices. That's still more than he'll ever spend so he should be doing something to reduce his taxable estate. However, Steve is so upset about his shrinking portfolio that he is reluctant to do very much estate tax planning.

The only move Steve has been willing to make, in order to reduce estate tax, is to put his house into a QPRT. After the trust term ends, the house will go to the trust beneficiaries, Steve's children. Assuming he survives the trust term, the house will be removed from his taxable estate while the delayed nature of the transfer will minimize gift taxes.

A QPRT may not be an ideal vehicle to be using when low interest rates reduce the gift-tax leverage you get with this type of trust. At the same time, the value of Steve's house is so high that he may not be getting a lot of future appreciation out of his estate. Nevertheless, Steve wanted to hold onto his investment portfolio. Getting his house out of his estate, by using a QPRT, was all that he was willing to do. In some cases, a little estate planning may be better than nothing.

Chapter 7
Doing Well While Doing Good

The expression "planned giving" generally covers charitable donations that are not outright contributions. Often, donors can receive recognition, lifetime income, and tax shelter.

To receive all of these advantages, you must be prepared to totally give up the assets you contribute. Those assets won't be available for bequests to the next generation. If you're willing to part with assets in this manner, here are some techniques to consider:

TAKE AND GIVE

Charitable Remainder Trusts allow donors (and, if desired, other individuals) to receive a stream of income while also making a charitable contribution, in the future. Taxes are deferred until the income is paid out to the designated recipient. The trust structure provides donors the opportunity to retain control over the funds after the gift has been made and to set the terms of the income payout.

Among Charitable Remainder Trusts, Charitable Remainder Annuity Trusts (CRATs) pay a fixed amount, at least 5% of the original contribution, to the income beneficiaries. A $1 million CRAT, for example, must pay out at least $50,000 per year. Larger payouts are possible, if the donor is more interested in lifetime income and less inclined to make a large donation when the trust remainder passes to charity.

By contrast, Charitable Remainder Uni-Trusts (CRUTs) pay the income beneficiaries a fixed percentage but a variable amount, at least 5% of the trust assets annually. It is possible to pay out a percentage higher than 5% but extremely large payouts (say, 50% per year) are prohibited.

Some donors prefer to use CRUTs and specify a low payout. If the trust assets earn 9% per year, for example, yet only 5% is paid out, the trust fund will grow. Over time, the income beneficiaries will be receiving 5% of a larger base so their absolute cash flow will increase.

Both CRATs and CRUTs have been used in planned giving strategies for many years. They are especially attractive when funded with appreciated assets because capital gains taxes may be deferred.

However, low interest rates may impede the formation of Charitable Remainder Trusts. For donors in their 40s and 50s, it may be difficult if not impossible to get meaningful income and still meet the "10% test."

Because of a change in tax law in the 1990s to stop perceived abuses, charitable remainder trusts must project at least a 10% charitable donation, once all the income beneficiaries have been paid. For young donors taking relatively high payouts, such a projection is not easy, and it's particularly difficult in a low interest-rate environment.

PUTTING CHARITY FIRST

On the other hand, low interest rates work in favor of Charitable Lead Trusts, which are the mirror image of remainder trusts. With a lead trust, income is paid to charity for the trust term. At termination, assets revert either to the donor, the donor's spouse, or to another trust beneficiary.

In the current environment, donors may prefer Charitable Lead Annuity Trusts (CLATs) rather than Charitable Lead Uni-Trusts (CLUTs). A CLAT pays a fixed amount to charity each year while a CLUT pays a fixed percentage of trust assets.

The lower the interest rate, the lower the discount rate used to put a present value on the distributions from the trust and the higher the present value of those distributions. You subtract the present value of the distributions from the initial transfer to get the value of the remainder interest, which is the taxable gift to the trust beneficiaries. At today's interest rates, it's easier to zero out a CLAT and thus avoid any gift tax consequences.

The IRS discount rate equals 120% of the annual mid-term applicable federal rate (AFR), rounded to the nearest 0.2%. When calculating the deduction earned by a planned gift, the discount rate for the month of the gift or for either of the two prior months may be used.

Here's how falling discount rates drop the gift tax on a CLAT, assuming a $1,000,000 transfer, a 15-year term, and a 9% ($90,000) annual payout to the charity.

Discount Rate	Present Value Of Charitable Gift	Taxable Gift
4.2%	$1,000,000	Zero
4.6%	$976,360	$23,640
5.2%	$939,460	$60,540

CLATs look a bit different today than they did a few years ago. These trusts should be funded with assets likely to produce a high return. Until recently, most people used stocks to fund the trust. Now you might want to use real estate instead. Income-producing properties may be donated to make the required payments. Normally, you'll save some complexity by transferring debt-free properties to these types of trusts.

PRIVATE, FIRST-CLASS

Rather than make outright gifts, you can make contributions to your own Private Family Foundation. Once the money is held in a private foundation, ongoing gifts can be made to selected charities.

Private foundations are subject to strict rules and regulations, including one that requires charitable contributions of at least 5% of assets per year. A foundation with $10 million in assets, for example, would have to donate at least $500,000 to qualified charities that year.

However, the directors of the foundation make those decisions, which can change from year to year. You and your relatives may sit on the board of directors, exercising control over the foundation's activities. Parents may see private foundations as vehicles for bringing the children together in the future, even if those children wind up in different places. The idea is that your family members will meet one or more times a year to make the decisions about charitable contributions.

Because of all the regulations, private foundations can be expensive and time-consuming to administer. Therefore, creating a private foundation generally will be worthwhile only if substantial amounts are contributed to establish it. At least $500,000 is suggested, and some experts would put the minimum considerably higher.

GRANT-FATHERED

You might not want to create a private foundation because of the time, money, and effort involved. Nevertheless, you may want to retain some control over your philanthropic efforts.

In such situations, contributions to a Donor-Advised Fund (DAF) may be desirable. Many financial institutions and community groups have established such funds. After a contribution has been made to a donor-advised fund, the donor may be able to make specific gifts to chosen charities over a period of years.

DAFs, long provided by local community foundations, in recent years also have been offered by major financial firms such as Fidelity, Vanguard, and Charles Schwab. In either form, donors make irrevocable gifts to the fund and claim an upfront deduction for the full value of the donated assets. After the contribution, the donor-advisor recommends to the sponsoring charity the amount and timing of gifts to various recipients. The actual charitable donations from the DAF (the "grants") may be spread over a period of years so clients retain the ability to submit grants from assets that they've already given away.

The relative strength of real estate vs. stocks is showing up in DAFs, which are receiving more contributions of real estate. You can have a property appraised, give it to the fund, and get a charitable deduction for the current value. With a private foundation, on the other hand, real estate deductions are limited to the cost basis, so that's a big advantage for donor-advised funds. After the contribution, the fund will sell the property and put the proceeds into your account, for subsequent grants to selected charities.

Compared with a private foundation, a DAF offers many of the advantages with less cost and complexity. After the donor's death, named beneficiaries–often the children–take over the advisory role. Then they can decide upon the charitable grants from the account, year after year.

Just as is the case with a private foundation, such a bequest can be more valuable than leaving the money outright. Not only can your children be given the opportunity to think beyond their own needs to the needs of others, they'll also benefit from future social connections. When other community members become aware of their grant-making powers, the children may enjoy tremendous upward mobility: they might be invited to serve on charitable and civic boards, for example.

After a DAF is set up, you keep control of the money, even though it has been irrevocably given away. If a charitable grant recipient adopts unwelcome policies, future grants can be directed elsewhere. Moreover, you can set parameters when they create the fund, reflecting your values. After your death, those parameters can remain in effect, influencing your children's future decisions.

Some DAFs offer further advantages. They may even prepare custom letterheads and personalized checks that say, for example,

"The John and Mary Smith Family Foundation." Then you can hand-deliver the checks, for maximum impact. In addition, you might prefer a foundation that's national in scope. If you donate money to a local community foundation, your children may wind up living in some other part of the country.

Regardless of whether a private foundation or a DAF is created, you can receive immediate tax benefits. A Charitable Lead Trust might be set up to fund a private foundation or DAF. In some circumstances, the trust assets can go to your children eventually, with minimal gift and estate tax consequences.

At the same time, a Charitable Remainder Trust can be set up to provide income to you or other family members upfront, with the trust assets going to your private foundation or to a DAF in the future. With such innovative planning, you and your family can have charitable donations coming and going, enjoying a myriad of tax benefits along the way.

THE ANNUITY ALTERNATIVE

Instead of donating through a charitable trust, you might prefer to fund a Charitable Gift Annuity. As the name suggests, you make a gift and receive an annuity, a stream of income that goes on for a lifetime. (Some charities stipulate a minimum amount for gift annuities, such as $10,000.) The older you are when you make the donation, the greater the income you can receive. A 60-year old donor might receive 5%, for example, or $5,000 per year on a $100,000 gift. An 80-year-old making that same $100,000 gift might receive 8%, or $8,000 per year.

Similarly, a couple will get lower payments than a single recipient. If that 80-year old donor has a 75-year-old spouse, and payments are to continue until they both die, the income might drop from 8% to 7% per year. In all of these situations, part of the income stream will be taxable while part will be a tax-free return of capital.

When gifts of appreciated assets are made, the capital gain obligation disappears. Donors get partial tax deductions as well: a couple, both aged 70, might get a deduction equal to 45% of the value of the asset they give away.

Gift annuities are especially popular among older, more conservative donors who like the stream of fixed income as well as the security. The obligation to pay the annuity is a claim on all the assets of the issuer.

If you prefer, Charitable Gift Annuities may be deferred. For instance, you might make a gift at age 55 but stipulate that annuity payments not begin until you reach 65. In that case, the payment stream will be greater, to take into account 10 years of growth in the interim.

With this strategy you may get a charitable deduction now, in a high tax bracket, yet defer the income until you're retired and your tax rate is lower.

ON THE HOUSE

One sophisticated strategy calls for combining a gift annuity with a future gift of a personal residence. Donating your house to a charity is relatively straightforward. You can retain the right to live in the house as long as you wish (tax professionals call this a "life interest") as well as the obligation to keep the house in good repair, pay property tax, etc. At your death, the house will pass to the charity.

Getting income from a gift annuity at the same time may be tricky, but it's possible. In essence, you'd have to find a charity that would be willing to guarantee you a life income because it is eager to receive your house eventually. The more valuable your home and the more desirable the location, the greater your chances of success. You'd have to negotiate terms with the charity; you'd probably want to be represented by an accountant and attorney as well. Some major not-for-profit organizations will enter into such agreements under the right circumstances.

For example, Sarah Johnson is a 70-year-old widow who owns a substantially appreciated second home worth $1 million on a nearby lakefront. If she holds onto it, it will be in her taxable estate. Selling it would generate income tax and the net proceeds would be subject to estate tax at her death.

Instead, she donated the house to a university, using a retained life estate gift annuity. She can use the house until she dies, after which it will go to the university.

Whenever you make a deferred gift to charity—including the future gift of your home—you'll get an immediate tax deduction. That deduction will be for a fraction of the value of your house, based on factors such as your age and the current interest rate climate.

Sarah Johnson, in this example, received an income tax deduction of nearly $250,000, which she can spread over the next six years, for the future charitable gift. She'll also get a lifetime annuity of around $30,000 per year while the value of the home will be excluded from her taxable estate.

Won't charities be leery of paying out $30,000 per year for an unknown number of years, under such an arrangement? Maybe, but maybe not. In the current climate, the charitable community is working harder to get pledges. Large institutions may be willing to enter into these types of agreements with donors who are 65 or older. Of course, the property involved must be one that's likely to remain desirable.

PLANNED GIVING

Private foundations and DAFs may be created while you are alive or they may go into effect at your death. In the latter role, they may be used as part of another sophisticated philanthropic technique: naming a charity as beneficiary of a tax-deferred retirement account. When a charity is named as retirement plan beneficiary, income and estate taxes can be avoided, so this is an effective way to make contributions.

This tactic has been helped by new IRS rules on minimum required distributions that were published in 2002. Formerly, designating a charity as an IRA beneficiary could be detrimental because distributions might be speeded up after the owner's death. That's no longer the case.

Under the new regulations, a charitable beneficiary can be cashed out while the other beneficiaries stretch out minimum required distributions. Suppose you have a $1 million IRA and you want to leave $250,000 to a particular charity. You could specify that $250,000 bequest on the beneficiary designation form.

Most forms have enough room for this type of arrangement; if not, the client can attach a separate sheet. After your death, your heirs will have until September 30th of the following year to pay $250,000 from the IRA to the charity. The balance of the IRA can be paid out over the life expectancies of the other beneficiaries.

Of course, one or two specified charities can be designated as IRA beneficiaries. Alternatively, you might name a private foundation or a DAF as the beneficiary.

NEW LIFE FOR IRA DONATIONS

As of this writing, proposed legislation would permit donors to make contributions directly from their IRAs without having to pay income tax. If such legislation is passed, as expected, certain philanthropic strategies that generally have been restricted to estate planning may become viable for lifetime gifts as well. IRA owners will be able to make direct rollovers to charity, tax-free. For the first time, it will become practical to include retirement assets in lifetime charitable planning.

Under current law, charitable intentions and IRAs don't mix well. Often, wealthy people would like to make generous charitable gifts. If those individuals have large IRAs, which is frequently the case, they may favor the idea of using IRA money for their donations.

However, traditional tax planning has called for IRA donations to be made as bequests rather than lifetime gifts.

Leaving a tax-deferred retirement account to an individual other than a spouse often means subjecting those funds to income tax, estate tax, and a generation-skipping transfer tax. Taken together, this triple tax may result in a tax burden approaching 80%. A $5 million IRA, for example, may be eroded by $4 million in taxes, leaving only $1 million for beneficiaries.

That same $5 million IRA, on the other hand, may pass intact to a charitable beneficiary. At the same time, assets not held in retirement plans may be left to children, grandchildren, and other loved ones, often with favorable tax consequences.

Unfortunately, money held in a tax-deferred retirement plan cannot be given directly to charity during the account owner's lifetime. Instead, funds must be withdrawn first, and such a withdrawal probably will be subject to income tax.

Thus, if you wish to donate $1 million to a favorite cause you might have to withdraw nearly $2 million from an IRA in order to do so. Federal, state, and possibly local income tax could amount to about 50% of the IRA withdrawal. As a result, few strategies for lifetime charitable giving have involved the use of retirement assets.

That could change, though, if the IRA Charitable Rollover is passed into law, as contemplated. Under one version of this proposed law, two forms of rollovers would be permitted:

- Donors who are at least age 59-1/2 would be able to rollover amounts from a traditional IRA or a Roth IRA to create a life income gift.
- Donors who are at least age 70-1/2 would be eligible to rollover amounts from a traditional IRA or a Roth IRA to make direct charitable gifts.

Thus, donors over age 70-1/2 could make either type of gift while those between ages 59-1/2 and 70-1/2 would be limited to life income gifts. In either case, no taxes would be due on the rollover. (No charitable deduction would be permitted, either, assuming the IRAs were funded with tax-deductible contributions.)

Thus, this proposed legislation would allow IRA owners over age 59-1/2 to use some or all of their IRAs to make life income gifts, with no tax consequences. Vehicles for life income gifts include Charitable Remainder Trusts and Charitable Gift Annuities.

Passage of such legislation also would permit individuals over 70-1/2 to make outright charitable donations from IRAs, tax-free. If you wanted to make a $1 million contribution to a university or a religious organization, for example, you could simply write a check from one account (an IRA) to another (the destination fund). Such contributions might provide a way to fulfill charitable commitments while keeping other assets in place.

FAMILY VALUES

In some cases, you may prefer to rollover IRA money to a private foundation rather than make an outright gift. You might want to use a sizable IRA for lifetime income, charitable contributions, and a valuable legacy to loved ones. Such an approach would call for a direct IRA rollover to a Charitable Remainder Trust. Instead of a public charity, though, the trust remainder could pass to your family foundation.

For example, suppose that you have most of your wealth tied up in shares of a closely held company, real estate, and an IRA. You want lifetime income for yourself and your spouse while also fulfilling your philanthropic inclinations. Your assets in this example, though, are largely illiquid.

If IRA Charitable Rollovers are permitted, you might decide to take your $2 million IRA and roll it over to a CRUT, tax-free, specifying a 5% payout to yourself and your spouse. Such payments would go on as long as either one of you is alive.

In this example, the income stream would start at $100,000 a year (5% of $2 million). If the trust assets grow faster than 5% per year, the lifetime payouts to you and to your surviving spouse will gradually increase. Distributions from the trust will be taxed as received.

At the death of your surviving spouse, the assets remaining in the trust might be $3 million, $4 million, or even greater, if the trust fund has been well managed. Those assets can pass to the John and Mary Smith Family Foundation, at that time. If proper planning has been done, no estate tax will be due on those assets.

The next generation of Smiths (and perhaps grandchildren or other loved ones) can be named as directors of this family foundation. Assuming a $4 million fund, the foundation will have to contribute at least $200,000 per year to a charity or charities. (If desired, you can establish some guidelines for charitable giving from the foundation.)

Again, if the assets are well managed, charitable donations from the foundation can go on indefinitely, rising with the asset base. Thus, your children and grandchildren, along with other descendants, can satisfy their own philanthropic intentions. They also will retain control and have a chance to establish relations with community and business leaders who are active in charitable causes.

Up until now, affluent donors have been advised to make contributions from taxable accounts during their lifetimes and to make charitable bequests from tax-deferred retirement plans. If IRA Charitable Rollover legislation is passed, planned giving will become more flexible. The traditional approach described above would still be valid but individuals would also be able to make lifetime contributions from IRAs, after certain age levels.

The expanded opportunities may allow you to increase charitable contributions, in many situations, while decreasing the amount going from an IRA to the IRS. Contributions may be relatively simple donations or they may involve highly complex strategies. Working with a knowledgeable advisor, you can design a plan with the ideal expected payout to yourself, your loved ones, and to your favored causes, while minimizing and deferring tax obligations.

Moreover, if you'd like to make a sizable charitable contribution, life insurance can help stretch your gift: relatively small premiums can produce a large death benefit for your favored cause. What's more, charitable gifts of life insurance can trim your taxable estate, avoid gift taxes, and generate current income deductions.

Suppose for the past 10 years you've paid $100,000 in premiums on a $1 million life insurance policy. You no longer need the insurance so you give it to a charity that will receive $1 million at your death. The policy can be removed from your taxable estate, no gift tax need be paid, and you can deduct the current value of the policy, typically the cash surrender or interpolated reserve value previously paid (subject to the limits on charitable deductions).

After you donate an insurance policy you can pay, and deduct, the annual premium. However, if you write a check directly to the insurance company, your deduction can't exceed 30% of your adjusted gross income (AGI) calculated before any net operating loss carry-back.

Instead, you should write a check for the premium amount to the charity that can remit the premium. Your contribution now will be deductible up to 50% of your AGI, as calculated above.

Chapter 8

Down With Estate Taxes

Your estate planning shouldn't revolve around tax planning but you shouldn't ignore estate taxes, either.

As of this writing, in 2004, everyone can leave unlimited amounts to a spouse and to charity, without generating an estate tax bill. In addition, you can leave up to $1.5 million worth of assets to other heirs, free of estate tax. That number is scheduled to increase in steps to $3.5 million, for people who die in 2009.

People who die in 2010 can leave any amount because the estate tax is scheduled to disappear. (There may be some income tax or capital gains on appreciated assets, though.) Then, beginning in 2011, the estate tax is supposed to reappear, with a $1 million exemption.

Naturally, there have been calls for Congress to clarify the situation, but what are the prospects? On the one side are proponents of repeal, who want the estate tax to be eliminated. As they see it, unless there's a permanent abolition of the "death tax," small business owners and family farmers will face a massive tax increase in 2011. Indeed, now that the Republicans control the House and the Senate, repeal is possible.

On the other hand, opponents of repeal counter that a stalemate is more likely. Although the Republicans control both chambers in Congress and may push through repeal, that won't necessarily be permanent. If repeal advocates win, opponents will come back and try to reinstate an estate tax.

A compromise may be reached, with an individual's estate tax exemption set anywhere from $1.5 million to $5 million and perhaps a top estate tax rate of 45%. Even if such a deal is concluded, though, it may hold only until the next time Congress takes a crack at the tax code.

PRESENT TENSE

How can you plan for this here today, gone tomorrow, back-the-day-after-tomorrow scenario? Your best option is to plan for the worst: anticipate death occurring in 2003, when the exemption is $1 million.

Now, $1 million may seem like a great deal but that doesn't mean $1 million of cash in the bank. At your death, your executor will add up all of your assets: investments, real estate, collectibles, retirement plans, etc. As mentioned, exemptions are allowed for bequests to your spouse and to charity; for all other assets, amounts in excess of $1 million are taxed at 41%-50%.

Say you leave a $400,000 IRA, a $400,000 house, and a $400,000 investment portfolio to your daughter. Your estate will total $1.2 million and over $80,000 in federal estate tax will be due.

To complicate matters, there is no knowing when you will die, how large an estate you'll leave, whether your heirs will need an inheritance, or what the tax laws will be at the time.

LEARNING YOUR A-Bs

As explained above, the federal estate tax might be gone tomorrow but it's still here today. In 2004, the federal estate tax exemption amount is $1.5 million; so many estate plans now call for a $1.5 million bequest to the decedent's children.

The problem, for many people, is that leaving $1.5 million to the children may cut into a surviving spouse's lifestyle. The solution, then, may be to leave that $1.5 million to a trust instead, naming the spouse as well as the children as beneficiaries. This technique uses the decedent's estate exemption and removes those assets from the survivor's estate but provides the widow with access to the funds, if necessary.

In the jargon of estate planning, this type of trust is a "B" trust, variously known as a bypass, family, or credit shelter trust. If there is a B trust, there must be an A trust, also known as a marital trust, because the surviving spouse is the beneficiary. Marital bequests may be outright but an A trust often is used to protect the survivor as well as the assets.

However, your estate plan should not blindly call for the exemption amount to go into the bypass trust. Suppose, for example, Bill Wilson dies in 2008 with a $2 million estate. If his plan calls for the exemption amount to go a B trust, that's it. The exemption amount that year will be $2 million, so all of Bill's estate will go to the B trust, leaving nothing for his surviving spouse to inherit.

That may not necessarily be a disaster. After all, Bill's surviving spouse still can get money from the B trust, as long as she's a beneficiary. Her access can be limited to providing for her health, education, support, or maintenance. That will cover most circumstances so her needs should be met.

If you have such a plan in place, and the B trust beneficiaries are just the children, you might want to re-evaluate your plan. Even if your surviving spouse is a beneficiary of the B trust, she may not have the same access to the assets as she would to the A trust assets, and certainly not as much as she would with an outright bequest.

There have to be some restrictions on the surviving spouse's access to the B trust in order to qualify for the tax benefits. For the survivor, there also may be a psychological disadvantages to having money held in the bypass trust.

That is, a widow may not place the same value on money in the B trust (designed to be outside of her taxable estate) as on money in the A trust ("her" trust), and she may not feel comfortable having to ask the B trustee for money she feels she should have inherited. Indeed, many people don't realize how stringent the trust terms can be.

This problem may not be as severe if the surviving spouse is the trustee of the B trust. If that's not feasible, she might be the co-trustee. Therefore, you may want to reconsider your choice for trustee of the B trust and consider including the surviving spouse.

WAIVING GOOD-BYE

Alternatively, you could create a B trust but fund it with only a token amount. Virtually everything else can be left to your surviving spouse, or to an A trust. Then, at your death, your survivor can disclaim (waive) whatever amount is suitable, to the B trust. This approach lets the survivor consider the tax law in effect at the time of death, the financial situation, and other factors, then make an informed decision.

By law, such a disclaimer must be made within nine months of the first death. By including the possible use of disclaimers in your estate plan, you may permit the survivor to shift assets to the first estate, where the tax rates are lower, and save significant amounts in tax. Your plan might provide that the survivor's executor can disclaim, within the nine-month period, if the survivor dies without disclaiming.

FLEX PLAN

In order for a tax-saving disclaimer to occur, you must build flexibility into your estate plan. After your death, your heirs can make the decisions that will lead to the lowest possible tax bill. Therefore, it is vital to educate your heirs so that they can act intelligently, when the time comes. A disclaimer may take one of several forms:

- Full disclaimer. An heir might waive an entire inheritance.
- Partial disclaimer. An heir might accept, say, the family residence but relinquish the inheritance of shares in a family business.

- Fractional disclaimer. The designated beneficiary of a $1 million IRA might accept, say, 25% ($250,000) and disclaim the other 75% ($750,000).

Where will disclaimed assets wind up? That depends on the contents of your will. Ideally, you should name backups in your will. If your spouse disclaims, the assets might be divided among your children.

Alternatively, the disclaimed assets might be transferred into an irrevocable trust you have established. In general, if you leave assets to a certain party and that party disclaims, the assets will be treated as if that party had predeceased you.

What happens if your will does not contain a contingency plan? Disclaimed assets will go into your residual estate. If your will does not specify recipients for such estate assets, they will be distributed as per state law.

HEIR TODAY, GONE TOMORROW

If handled correctly, a disclaimer can be a valuable tax saver. Say you leave $1 million to your daughter Joan. By the time you die, though, Joan is wealthy in her own right. If she accepts this inheritance, she'll receive money she doesn't really need and possibly swell her future estate tax bill.

Instead, Joan disclaims. Under your will, her daughter Janice, your granddaughter, winds up with a $1 million inheritance. Those assets will not be subject to estate tax at Joan's death.

However, when assets are disclaimed and the recipient is a grandchild or great-grandchild, the generation skipping transfer (GST) tax may be triggered. In 2003, each person had a $1.1 million exemption from this tax but larger amounts must be factored into disclaimer strategies.

Despite GST issues, a disclaimer strategy might be especially popular among wealthy couples. Suppose William Benson died in

2003 with a $10 million estate, which he left to his wife Nancy. Not only did Nancy disclaim $1 million, which will pass to their children, exempt from estate tax, she disclaimed another $500,000, which will be taxed at relatively low estate tax rates.

The 2001 tax law makes it even more important to build flexibility into your estate plan. An inflexible estate plan can have unfortunate consequences. Suppose that you anticipate that the estate tax would be repealed so you simply leave everything to your surviving spouse. However, at your death, the estate tax is in effect and likely to remain so. Thus, your surviving spouse's estate faces a hefty tax bill, in the future.

Instead, your estate plan should allow your survivor to disclaim so that assets pass to your children, using the current estate tax exemption to avoid a tax payment. This will reduce the taxable estate and the amount of estate tax your children eventually will owe. However, if the assets pass to your children, your survivor will have no chance to benefit from the disclaimed assets. They might be better off if your will had provided for disclaimed assets to go into a bypass trust, as explained above.

WIN-WIN SITUATION

Building flexibility into your estate plan can provide for your loved ones, no matter how taxes might change in the future. Say you live for another 40 years, gradually spending down your assets. At the time of your death, you leave $200,000 to your daughter, an amount too small to be affected by estate taxes. Your daughter accepts this modest inheritance and no problems arise.

On the other hand, say you die with a $2 million estate. Again, if the estate exemption is $5 million, your daughter can inherit without any tax problems.

Suppose, though, that you leave $2 million and the estate tax exemption, at the time of your death is $1 million. Your daughter, in the meantime, has prospered in her own career and in her investments so she has considerable wealth on her own. If she accepts your inheritance, she'll be receiving money she doesn't need. If she invests that money and it continues to grow, she may be creating or expanding the estate tax payable at her death. In this situation, she can disclaim her right to her inheritance.

If the idea of this flexibility seems appealing to you, how should you set up your estate plan? You might provide that any disclaimed assets will go to your daughter's two children, your grandchildren. Assuming they are capable young adults, this might be an acceptable plan. As mentioned, there currently is a 50% GST tax on bequests to grandchildren, but you can leave up to $1.1 million worth of assets, exempt from the GST.

In reality, though, your situation might not be so clear-cut. Your grandchildren might be minors, or they might be adults who are vulnerable to predators, bad marriages, and so on. In essence, you may be reluctant to see them receive large amounts of money outright. Moreover, when the time comes to disclaim assets, your daughter might be reluctant to give them away, for fear she'll need them some day.

Often, the best solution is for you to provide that a trust be created, with your daughter as well as your grandchildren (and perhaps other loved ones) as trust beneficiaries. If your daughter decides to disclaim to such a trust, the transfer of assets to the trust can use up your estate tax exemption and remove the assets from your daughter's estate.

Nevertheless, the trustee can distribute assets to your daughter, if it becomes necessary, or to your grandchildren. In the meantime, trust assets may be out of the reach of creditors, divorcing spouses, etc. The same GST tax will apply to this type of bequest, and the same $1.1 million exemption will be available.

PLANNING AHEAD

While you're creating this type of sophisticated estate plan, don't overlook your IRA or other tax-deferred retirement plans. Such assets won't be affected by whatever you have in your will; instead, they'll pass to beneficiaries you name on a special form for each account.

Often, your spouse will be the designated beneficiary. But if you're not currently married of if your spouse has sufficient assets, you might name a child as the beneficiary of your retirement account. Again, you can name your grandchildren or a trust as contingent beneficiaries of your IRA.

After your death, your children will have nine months to decide whether they'll need the IRA. If not, they can disclaim the inherited IRA to a trust, with your grandchildren as trust beneficiaries. The trustee can make sure that distributions are stretched out over your grandchildren's long life expectancies.

Suppose, for example, that your daughter inherits your IRA when she is 58. She can take minimum distributions over a life expectancy of 27 years. On the other hand, if your daughter's son inherits (outright or in trust), at age 20, he will have 63 years to stretch out distributions: an extra 36 years. Unless your daughter truly needs the money in the IRA, it makes sense for her to disclaim in favor of your grandson–and you should have an estate plan in place that will make this all possible.

Again, leaving an IRA to a grandchild will trigger the GST tax, but again you can use a $1.1 million GST exemption. What's more, these numbers are scheduled to change in the future and there undoubtedly will be further legislation in this area. Therefore, you should work with an attorney who's experienced in wills and trusts in order to create a flexible plan, and you need to check back with your attorney every few years to see if your plan needs updating.

Just as important, you need to explain your plan to all the heirs and backup heirs, so they understand what you've done–and what they need to do after you're no longer able to make plans for your loved ones.

CASCADING BENEFICIARY DESIGNATION PLAN

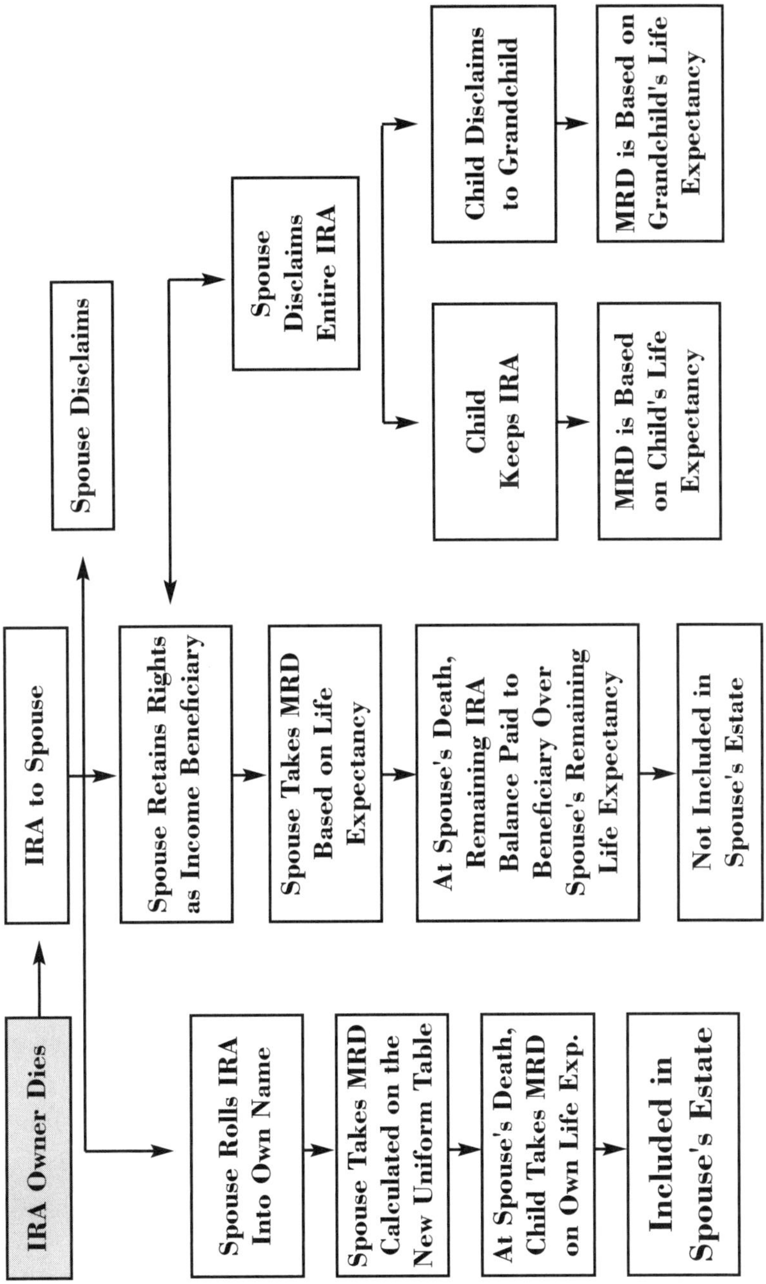

DOWNPLAYING DISCLAIMERS

Adding disclaimers to your estate plan adds flexibility but you should not rely upon them exclusively. Often, if an advisor suggests that a widow disclaim some assets, she may hear, "You've lost your husband, now lose some of your money." Especially for elderly people, the idea of disclaiming part of their inheritance can be a foreign concept.

There may be technical problems with disclaimers, too. You can't disclaim an asset after you've enjoyed a benefit from it. If a widow has cashed a $12 dividend check, she can't disclaim the stock. Thus, you should explain your estate plan thoroughly to the interested parties. Point out the huge tax savings that a disclaimer may generate–and warn them not to tap assets they might want to disclaim.

Another possibility is that an heir won't be capable of understanding that disclaiming certain assets can lead to tax savings. As people age, it becomes increasingly important that they name someone to act on their behalf, via a durable power of attorney. Such powers should explicitly authorize the agent to disclaim inheritances, if that appears to be a wise choice.

If disclaimers have so many disadvantages, what other techniques might be included in your estate plan?

- Percentage caps. You need some mechanism for preventing an overload in the B trust. For example, you might plan for the exemption amount to go into a B trust, but not more than half of your estate. If you leave $2 million worth of assets, $1 million can go into the bypass trust, so it won't be taxed in your survivor's estate, while the other half can go to your spouse.
- Absolute caps. You might put a $1 million (or lower) limit on the amount that goes into a bypass trust.
- Sole-beneficiary B trust. You might fund the bypass trust to the amount of the estate tax exemption and name your spouse as the sole beneficiary. This would help to provide for

your spouse, yet assets in a carefully drafted bypass trust would be out of the survivor's estate. Your children might be secondary trust beneficiaries, to inherit after your spouse's death.

- Minimum B trust funding. You might fund the bypass trust with a minimum amount, perhaps $400,000. Then you'll know that at least some money will go into the bypass trust, out of the survivor's taxable estate. Your surviving spouse can be given the power to disclaim additional assets, to the bypass trust, up to the exemption amount.
- Double B trusts. Another strategy would be to split the estate tax exemption of the first spouse to die between two bypass trusts. One trust could be solely for the benefit of your surviving spouse while the other trust could have multiple beneficiaries, including your surviving spouse. You'd rely upon the trustee to sprinkle distributions to the other beneficiaries.

For now and for the immediate future, such planning makes sense mainly for couples with estates up to $3 million. Larger estates, especially those much larger, will probably be able to fully utilize the estate tax exemption at the first death and still leave ample amounts for the surviving spouse.

Changing the character of the A-B trust may have other implications. Traditionally, the bypass trust has been managed for growth and the marital trust for income. If your surviving spouse is dependent upon the assets in the bypass trust, a different approach might be needed. That approach might be the use of a "total return trust," managed for growth but tapped for income (see below).

STATES' RIGHTS

Another factor to consider is state law. Leaving too much to a bypass trust might run afoul of laws in certain states that require a surviving spouse to inherit at least a specified portion of the other spouse's estate.

Moreover, enacted and proposed federal tax changes will effectively reduce state tax revenues, and every state is likely to react in a different way to recapture the lost income. Therefore, when trusts are created, someone–perhaps the trustee or a trust protector–should be given the power to change the domicile of the trust. Depending on how state laws change, the trust could move to a state where the overall tax burden would be reduced.

Using trusts in estate planning may become more complex but they should not be abandoned. Trusts serve so many purposes, from asset protection to probate avoidance, that they will remain essential planning tools.

As for taxes, uncertainty about future legislation is nothing new–and it should not be an excuse for procrastination. Your estate plan should allow for deaths to occur right away, because that might happen. Then you can meet with your advisors to review your plan each year, to make sure it's still valid.

Tax law may change dramatically in the years before your death. In addition, you can't know how your loved ones will fare in the future. They may lose a fortune in an ongoing bear market or enjoy a robust rebound.

For all of these reasons, it's vital to build flexibility into your will and any trust documents. Give your heirs the chance to enjoy all of your assets, but also construct a succession plan in case they can save taxes with discerning disclaimers.

REMARRIED, WITH CHILDREN

Your estate planning may be even more complicated if you are remarried, with children from a previous marriage. In this situation it may not be likely that your surviving spouse will disclaim, in favor of your own children, and it might be awkward for your survivor as well as those children to be beneficiaries of the B trust.

Some unique advantages are possible–and some unique concerns arise–when the A (marital) trust is designed to become a Qualified

Terminable Interest Property (QTIP) trust. Trust income must be distributed to the surviving spouse; no one else may have any access to the money. However, at the death of the surviving spouse the trust assets will be distributed to beneficiaries chosen by the trust creator.

Such trusts are especially valuable if you're remarried, with children from a previous marriage. You can provide a lifetime income to your surviving spouse yet still have your assets wind up with your own children. In the meantime, assets left to the QTIP trust won't be subject to estate tax until the second death.

In some situations, a QTIP trust may prove to be awkward if your surviving spouse lives for many years, deferring your children's inheritance. Thus, you might want to leave some money to your children at your death, directly or in trust or through a life insurance policy.

BALANCING ACT

In some QTIP situations, the widow Nancy may be a spendthrift who wants the trustee to load up on bonds, in order to provide her with ample current cash flow, while her stepson Phil might prefer to see the trust funds invested in stocks for long-term appreciation. Satisfying all the parties is especially demanding in today's low-yield climate. If a trustee wants to provide the beneficiaries with current income of 5% or 6%, virtually all of the portfolio might have to be invested in fixed-income vehicles, sacrificing growth. Alternatively, a trust fund invested in stocks may provide little current income.

Moreover, until recently the "prudent man" rule inhibited investments by trustees. Under that formula, each individual investment was judged by whether or not it was prudent, so small-cap stocks or junk bonds might have been forbidden. In recent years, most states have adopted some form of the "prudent investor" rule. This rule, based on modern portfolio theory, states that the entire portfolio must be invested prudently; thus, various asset classes can be mixed in an effort to optimize results.

The prudent investor rule may put even more pressure on trustees to invest wisely, so trustees need to know about asset allocation and tax-efficient investing. If the trustee is not sophisticated in those areas, it may be mandatory to name a qualified professional to help manage the portfolio.

A savvy investment pro, then, can manage a QTIP trust as a total return trust. As the name suggests, these trusts instruct the trustee to invest for overall return rather than bifurcating a portfolio into income and growth segments. Such trusts may be heavily weighted towards equities, which have been long-term winners, so current income might be only 1% or 2% per year, hardly enough to satisfy income-oriented trust beneficiaries.

To avoid slighting these beneficiaries, a total return trust might pay out a certain percentage of trust assets per year, even if some of that cash flow must come from selling securities. A $100,000 trust fund that pays out $5,000 (5%) might increase in value to $110,000 the next year, in which case the income beneficiary's 5% payout would increase to $5,500. (Because these trusts resemble Charitable Remainder Uni-Trusts, described previously, they are sometimes referred to as "private uni-trusts.")

In these circumstances, the trust beneficiaries have compatible rather than conflicting interests. The income beneficiary will receive a stream of cash flow that may grow over time, as long as the total return exceeds the payout rate, and the remainder men (the beneficiaries who'll eventually inherit the money) will wind up with a trust fund larger than the original amount.

CALMING THE CASH FLOW

If a total return trust seems to be attractive, some practical issues should be addressed. For one, what will be the asset base for the purpose of calculating the required distribution? If it's simply the year-end trust value, income to the trust beneficiaries may fluctuate wildly: the payout can decline if the securities in the trust lose value.

For example, a $100,000 trust might be worth $70,000 or even $60,000 the next year, in the case of a severe bear market. To smooth out the flow of income, the distributions might be based on a three-year or a five-year average of year-end trust values.

Another concern is the proper level of the trust payout. The principal can build if the payout rate is low; it's also possible to structure this type of trust so that the payout percentage starts low and then increases in later years.

Some experts assert that a trust rate of 3.5%-4% may be appropriate in some situations while a "give-me-five" strategy may work well in others. Suppose, for example, a decedent leaves $1 million to a credit shelter trust for a surviving spouse and the children while other assets go into a marital trust. As long as the spouse doesn't need the income from the credit shelter trust, that trust can be allowed to grow for the benefit of the children.

In these circumstances, the trust documents might specify a percentage of the trust assets, not to exceed 5%, and give the surviving spouse the right to withdraw that percentage during a certain time period each year. The survivor can allow this right to lapse if the funds aren't needed. Then the money can stay in the trust, accumulating for the future, without adverse gift or estate tax consequences.

PERFECT FIT

The concept of a total return trust might seem ideal for QTIP trusts. As mentioned, the surviving spouse is entitled to all of the trust's income, which enables the trust to qualify for the marital deduction from estate tax. At the surviving spouse's death, the trust fund passes to beneficiaries named by the first spouse to die.

However, QTIP trusts may create tension between the income beneficiary and the remainder men. The tension may be even greater if the surviving spouse is the product of a remarriage and the ultimate beneficiaries are from the decedent's first marriage.

Can a total return trust ease the strain a QTIP trust places on the trustee? Unfortunately, tax law may get in the way. In these trusts the surviving spouse is entitled to all of the net income annually, not to some arbitrary uni-trust amount.

One possible solution is to structure the trust so that the surviving spouse is entitled to all of the net income from the trust or a uni-trust percentage, whichever is greater. Some professionals caution that this strategy may not work, though. There is always a chance that the surviving spouse will challenge the arrangement, saying that the income amount isn't adequate.

The outcome of such a suit will be uncertain, varying from state to state, and you may not want to take the risk. If you set the uni-trust amount high enough to minimize the trustee's exposure, the uni-trust may not accomplish what it was designed to do.

Other professionals disagree, saying that such an approach might make things easier for a trustee caught in the middle between battling beneficiaries. After all, in today's climate–Treasury bond yields are under 5%, in 2003—a uni-trust paying 5% would seem to be treating the income beneficiary well.

Therefore, it seems that some details need to be ironed out before total return trusts become a staple in estate planning. Attorneys are just beginning to become familiar with these trusts, which have been created in response to the frustrations expressed by many trustees.

PITFALL OF QTIP AS IRA BENEFICIARY

Your surviving spouse might live so long that most or all of your IRA will be paid out, leaving little or nothing to charity. This problem is unique to situations where an IRA is left to a QTIP, as the measuring life expectancy for your surviving spouse is calculated at actual life expectancy, not at the more favorable new Uniform Table.

HOPEFUL SIGNS

So far, attorneys have been slow to adopt these trusts, perhaps because they require more explanation to their clients. One approach would be to express the hope that a certain payout would be maintained but to avoid any requirement. That would suggest to the trustee that principal invasion might be appropriate.

Thus, the trust documents may need to define total return and indicate how it can be achieved. This may mean carrying over a lifetime investment strategy to a trust fund for the heirs.

Besides total return trusts, there are other ways to avoid hard feelings in estates that use QTIP trusts for estate tax deferral:

- Outright gifts to the children may be help.
- Another solution is to buy life insurance so some heirs get an immediate payoff, rather than waiting years for someone else to die.
- If an estate is large enough, multiple trusts can be created, tailored to the needs of different beneficiaries.
- If there's a family business, heirs who need income might be made preferred shareholders.

Working with a skilled professional who truly knows your family, you may be able to come up with solutions that work in the "real world." Every family is different.

WHEN LESS IS GREATER

In estate planning, the sum of the parts may be less than the whole. This apparent paradox can lead to huge tax savings–with the blessing of the IRS.

Recent developments have generated a strategy that's especially effective for transferring a closely held family business to the next generation. The same strategy also can be applied to other assets, such as real estate and partnership interests.

To see how this plan might work, suppose that Ted Parker builds a company worth $2.5 million. He dies holding 90% of the shares, which he leaves to his wife Jean. (No estate tax is due on marital bequests.) By the time Jean dies, her shares in the company are worth $3 million. At a 45% federal estate tax rate, those shares are taxed at $1.35 million. To satisfy the IRS, their children may have to borrow heavily or even sell the company.

Suppose that Ted's brother Bob builds another company that's also worth $2.5 million. He also dies with 90% of the shares. However, instead of an outright bequest to his wife Lois, Bob leaves her 45% and leaves the other 45% to a QTIP trust. Property left to a QTIP trust avoids estate tax so no estate tax is due at Bob's death.

When Lois dies years later, the value of the company is over $3 million. Nominally, the 45% share she owns outright is worth about $1.5 million but an appraisal might value this block of stock at only $1 million. Similarly, the 45% held in the QTIP trust might be valued at $1 million. In this case the total value of those shares is $2 million, not $3 million, and federal estate tax savings of $450,000 result.

How does a $3 million asset merit a $2 million valuation? A minority interest in a closely held company is not worth its pro rata share of the business. Minority owners lack control; often, they have a difficult time finding willing buyers.

Thus, a third-party buyer is unlikely to pay $900,000 for a 45% share in a business valued at $2 million. Such a buyer might pay $630,000, which would be a 30% discount from nominal value, or $720,000, a 20% discount, or some other amount. On the other hand, a 90% interest in that same company might be sold for $1.8 million or even more, given the control such a holding would confer.

The question, then, in the Bob-Lois example is whether the shares held by Lois and those held for her benefit in a QTIP trust must be combined, for valuation purposes. There have been several court cases affirming the principle that shares held outright and shares held in trust won't be aggregated. After contesting these cases, and losing, the IRS finally gave in.

PREMIUM OR DISCOUNT?

The final straw for the IRS might have been the case involving Frederick Mellinger (Frederick's of Hollywood) and his wife Harriet. Frederick left a 28% interest in the company to a QTIP trust while Harriet held another 28%.

At Harriet's death, the shares were appraised at around $7 apiece. Her estate claimed a 31% minority discount for the 28% interest she held, valuing the shares at $4.79 apiece.

Similarly, the 28% interest in the QTIP trust was valued at $4.79 per share. (Although Frederick's of Hollywood stock was publicly traded, the blocks at issue here were so large that disposition on the public market would have disrupted trading.)

The IRS claimed both blocks of stock were owned by Harriet's estate: all of the shares were included in her taxable estate, subject to estate tax at the same time. Because the total added up to 56%, the IRS added a control premium, putting the value at $8.46 per share.

The Tax Court disagreed with the IRS. The QTIP shares might be included in Harriet's estate, for tax purposes, but she didn't really control them–she couldn't sell them, for example.

The QTIP shares had to be distributed as per Frederick's instructions. Thus, the Tax Court viewed these holdings as two separate blocks of stock, each representing only 28% of the company–and each entitled to a minority discount. In this case, that discount was put at 25% from appraised value, giving Harriet's estate most of the tax advantages it had claimed.

SUBTRACT, DON'T ADD

This defeat was not the first the IRS had lost on this issue. In a string of cases with similar fact patterns, the IRS had asserted that both blocks of shares should be aggregated because they're both included in the surviving spouse's taxable estate.

In the Mellinger case, the Tax Court found that the two blocks of stock should not be aggregated for valuation purposes. Under the QTIP rules, the surviving spouse did not control the shares, which had to pass to beneficiaries named by the first spouse to die. Each block was considered a separate entity and sizable minority discounts were approved.

This Tax Court decision added weight to a similar result from the Fifth Circuit Court of Appeals in the 1996 Bonner case (which involved real estate), as well as other cases. Indeed, in 1999 the IRS formally agreed to accept Bonner, Mellinger, and the other cases as precedents.

Now that the IRS has thrown in the towel, you can adopt this technique with confidence. Leaving assets to a QTIP provides most of the benefits of an outright bequest to a surviving spouse: estate tax deferral, lifetime income for the survivor, and access to principal in case of an emergency. Moreover, the trust assets will pass to beneficiaries designated by the first spouse to die.

The surviving spouse probably can be the trustee of the QTIP trust, and the trust will still be treated as a separate entity for purposes of determining the ownership of the assets. You need to work with a local attorney when making such decisions because state laws may vary.

POWER PLAY

Planning to take advantage of this strategy may involve other arrangements. For example, a QTIP trust must pay income to the surviving spouse yet many family businesses don't pay dividends. This could lead to a denial of the QTIP trust's tax advantages and an acceleration of estate tax.

One tactic you might consider: give the surviving spouse the power to force the trustee to sell the shares and reinvest in income-producing assets. The survivor does not have to use this power but its presence may deter an IRS challenge.

Of course, it's vital for the surviving spouse to have sufficient income from other sources, especially if the shares in the family business don't pay dividends, which often will be the case.

IN ORDER OF DISAPPEARANCE

Another concern: it's impossible to know for certain which spouse will die first. In the above Bob-Lois example, the estate plan will work if Bob dies first but, if Lois is the first to die, Bob will be stuck with a majority interest in the family business.

Thus, it may make more to sense split the shares while both spouses are alive, making sure neither one will die with a 50%-or-greater interest. To split the shares, one spouse can make a lifetime gift to the other with no gift tax consequences.

This approach generally works best if the assets are going to be left to the spouse anyway. Even in those situations, though, you need to be ready to give up some control over your assets, which isn't always easy to do. Most of all, you need to incorporate such tactics into an overall succession plan.

For example, some provision must be made for ongoing management of a family business, if most of the shares are going to be owned by the surviving spouse or a QTIP trust. Transferring some stock to the new managers is probably a good idea. In some companies, though, stock ownership is restricted to family members. If you want to bring in outside managers and motivate them, some type of a phantom stock plan might be appropriate.

In any case, the earlier such a strategy is in place, the better. If you wait until a surviving spouse is left with 80% of the shares in his or her name, planning will be more difficult. Even then, don't give up. As long as you can re-shuffle assets to keep any one person's ownership below 50%, valuation discounts may be available. This is a simple, effective technique that's been approved by the IRS so it's worth exploring before venturing into areas that may create problems.

Chapter 9

Survivor: Reality Show For Surviving Spouses

The facts of life inevitably give way to the facts of death. Women not only have longer life expectancies than men, they usually are younger than their husbands. As a result, widows are far more common than widowers.

In the U.S., a wife will outlive her husband by seven years on average. During those seven years (or a longer time period, in many cases), widows must manage inherited assets, which may be considerable. Although there are exceptions, many of these widows have not had experience handling the family's finances. As they age and their health declines, widows may face severe challenges maintaining their own lifestyle and preserving an inheritance for future generations.

That may change in the future because many young and middle-aged women have more education and more workplace experience than their mothers and grandmothers. For many of today's female 60-somethings and 70-somethings though, handling their money can be a daunting challenge.

To minimize the risks, couples might put necessary support services in place while both spouses are alive.

- Arrangements can be made so that income from Social Security checks, pensions, and investments will be directly deposited into an appropriate bank account.
- Similar arrangements can be made for automatic transfers to pay bills that recur each month.

- Setting up a central assets account at a financial institution may make it easier to track checking and savings accounts as well as selected securities.

Even if such safeguards are in place, most widows will benefit from expert assistance. A widow's accountant, attorney, and insurance professional can form a team to help her understand her situation and make appropriate recommendations.

Better yet, financial education should begin when both spouses are still alive and in good health. Both spouses should know in advance what must be done, after the first death. The spouse who handles money the least should know what assets will be available, and how to find them. No one should automatically assume that the survivor will find everything in order.

ENSURING INSURANCE

While both spouses are alive, it's vital that life insurance policies be checked carefully. In case of a remarriage, for example, you'll want to be sure that the policy's beneficiary is the current spouse, not the ex.

Generally, it's best to hold a life insurance policy in trust, with the trust named as the beneficiary. Properly done, this removes the insurance proceeds from the decedent's taxable estate. Also, the trust documents can dictate how those proceeds shall be used.

It's true that insurance proceeds will escape estate tax should the policy be owned by another party such as a grown son or daughter. However, such a tactic may have tragic results.

Take the case of Peter Fulton, whose life was insured under a policy owned by his daughter. Unfortunately, Peter's daughter died and her husband inherited her assets, including this policy.

This widower remarried and he, too, predeceased Peter, leaving the policy to his second wife. In the meantime, Peter had become uninsurable and could not obtain more coverage.

As a result, when Peter ultimately died a woman with no connection to his family collected a hefty amount of life insurance, tax-free. Peter's heirs faced an equally hefty estate tax bill, with no insurance proceeds to pay what they owed.

DISCLAIMER PLANNING

Such disasters can be avoided by thoughtful planning. Moreover, if a couple's affairs are in order, a widow won't be under as much pressure to handle financial matters right away. That's not always the case, though. Some investment, legal, and tax decisions can't be put off so widows have to make some crucial decisions within that one-year time frame.

On the estate planning side, a widow has nine months to disclaim any unneeded assets. If such assets aren't disclaimed, they may wind up in the survivor's estate, subject to estate tax. Given the proper planning, disclaimed assets may be passed to a descendant or to a trust, out of the widow's taxable estate.

The same nine-month deadline also applies to estate tax returns, which must be filed if the decedent's gross estate (valued on the date of death) plus taxable lifetime gifts exceed the exclusion amount for the year of death–$1.5 million in 2004. On the other hand, the so-called "alternate valuation date" is six months (not nine months) after the date of death. That is, an estate can choose to value assets six months after death, if that would result in a lower estate tax bill than a date-of-death valuation. However, all the assets in an estate must be valued on the same date; you can't pick and choose the low-value dates, asset by asset.

Of course, a tax professional (probably the same person who prepared the decedent's tax returns) will be responsible for observing these deadlines. Nevertheless, a widow should be prepared to make sure that her tax professional is up to speed on these issues.

OPTION PLAYS

Other issues must be addressed in a timely manner. The tax-deferral of the decedent's retirement plan needs to be maintained, for example. The surviving spouse can roll the account balances over to an IRA and name new beneficiaries (such as a child or children). After the surviving spouse dies, the children can stretch required distributions over their life expectancies, per the IRS tables.

A widow may also inherit a deferred annuity (fixed or variable). In these cases, the tax code provides several possibilities. However, insurance companies and other issuers may not offer all of these options to beneficiaries.

1. One option that's usually available is taking the amount of the contract in a lump-sum. With this choice, though, you'll owe all the deferred income tax right away.
2. You may be able to "annuitize" the contract, which assures you of a fixed stream of income over your lifetime. This income will be part taxable and part tax-free; payments must begin within one year of the contract owner's death.
3. A third option may be available to widows and widowers, who can take over the contract from a deceased spouse and keep the annuity in place, extending the tax-deferral.
4. You can choose to receive the amount of the contract within five years of the owner's death, rather than right away. This payout can be taken periodically or postponed until the five-year mark. As the money is received, income tax will be due. This option may be the most attractive for non-spouses because it offers the greatest amount of tax-deferral.

Some annuity issuers will assume that a surviving spouse will continue the contract unless otherwise notified. For non-spouses, the company may make a lump-sum payout unless another option is chosen within 60 days of the contract owner's death. If you inherit a deferred annuity, you should read the contract carefully to see what options you have and how soon you must act.

PRESERVING PROTECTION

An inherited IRA or annuity may offer more than tax-deferral. Such accounts may be protected from creditors, under state law. A few states specifically protect IRA owners as well as individual beneficiaries from the claims of creditors (some extend this protection to annuities as well).

Most states, though, don't spell out this protection. If there is no specific protection, how safe is an inherited IRA? That may depend upon the type of claim.

1. Claims against the decedent, the original owner of the IRA. IRA beneficiaries probably won't be liable for those claims. However, any taxes owed to the IRS will have to be paid.
2. Claims against the IRA beneficiary. Suppose Jane Smith inherits an IRA from her husband and causes a tragic auto accident. Can the inherited IRA be tapped to pay any damages? Except in those few states with specific protection, that's an open question. However, it's likely that the IRA could be vulnerable, if Jane's insurance is inadequate.

If that's the situation for individual IRA beneficiaries, what happens when the IRA beneficiary is a trust?

That's a matter of state law. However, if the language of the trust says, "debts shall be paid," mandating repayment, the trustee may be obligated to withdraw funds from the IRA or use other assets that were otherwise protected from creditors by state law.

The bottom line, then, is that anyone who wants to name a trust as IRA beneficiary must pay careful attention to the drafting of that trust.

If the trust doesn't permit debts of the decedent to be paid, the beneficiary may well enjoy creditor protection; the same probably will be true if the trust is silent on this issue. In fact, a trustee who pays debts of the decedent from an IRA when not specifically instructed to do so may be charged with a breach of fiduciary duties and incur liability.

On the other hand, if the trust says that "debts of the decedent shall be paid," the creditor-proof status of the IRA probably would be destroyed. Again, some savvy planning by couples may save the survivor a great deal of grief.

AVOIDING FINAL JEOPARDY

Regardless of what transpired before the first death, though, one of the first things a widow should do is review estate planning documents, which may need to be revised to adjust to new circumstances. Besides an updated will, estate planning for a widow might call for a durable power of attorney, a health care proxy, and a living will.

Estate planning will be further complicated if a widow remarries. In that case, a properly-executed prenuptial agreement may protect the widow herself as well as her children and grandchildren.

Gifting strategies should also be considered. Under current law, it may make financial sense for wealthy widows to give gifts to family members as a way to reduce future estate tax. Everybody, including widows, can give up to $11,000 per year to any number of recipients without triggering a gift tax.

In addition, direct payments for someone else's health and education enjoy a gift tax exclusion. The more money a widow gives away, the less will be left in her taxable estate—and the smaller the estate tax obligation.

Such gifts may be appropriate if the widow's net worth is well over the estate-tax exemption amount ($1.5 million in 2004). However, for widows who are under that threshold or even slightly over it, gifts may not be appropriate.

Such widows might be better off spending down–and enjoying–their own money. They can travel or spend money on comfortable retirement housing, thereby eliminating any estate tax problem. Only in cases of extreme wealth, where there is more money than a widow could reasonably spend, does giving away assets make sense.

ADVISE AND PROTECT

While a widow is establishing an estate plan, should she consult with her grown children? Not necessarily. Some widows prefer to manage their own finances. They see an obvious conflict of interest: while a widow might want to spend money on her own well-being, her children may want her to spend less and thus preserve their inheritance. A widow might want to live in an expensive assisted living facility, for example, even if that means spending down her inherited wealth.

As a result, some widows actually may need financial protection from their children. That protection, in turn, may be provided by a reliable financial advisor.

What can a widow do when her son Bob wants $50,000 to buy a sports car? When her daughter Barbara requests $100,000 to remodel her kitchen? Chances are, a widow might feel guilty about saying no, and her children may resent any refusal.

That's where a trustworthy advisor may be invaluable. He or she can meet with Bob and Barbara and say, "I'm familiar with your mother's financial circumstances. She can't afford to give you that kind of money because she may need those funds to pay her own bills some day."

With this strategy, the widow can avoid family dissension. The advisor becomes the "bad guy," turning down requests for money, but that advisor's expertise will make the refusal credible.

Of course, there are all manner of predators likely to seek out wealthy widows, not just relatives. A trusted advisor, along with some financial education, can be the most effective form of "shark repellent."

JAWS 2004

Unfortunately, some advisors turn out to be the sharks. In one case, a 77-year-old widow of a preacher went to a broker for help. The broker put her into a market timing program, venture capital funds, and biotech stocks. When the market crashed in 2000, the widow was destitute.

In a similar situation, a 75-year-old widow living in a nursing home was in poor health. She told her broker, who worked for a major firm, that she wanted her son to have a power of attorney. The power wasn't delivered for over a year; subsequently, the son's requests to see his mother's brokerage account statements were ignored. When the mother died and the son realized how the account had declined, he filed a complaint against the broker.

In 1999, this widow's portfolio was 85% in high-tech stocks and 15% in bonds. By 2000, there were no bonds at all. The broker did not seem to have done anything to get the portfolio to generate income, even though this widow had needed $3,000 a month to pay her nursing home bills. Again, the 2000-2002 bear market just about wiped out her portfolio.

With these sorts of experiences in mind, it's best if a couple seeks out advisors who can be trusted to provide prudent counsel to a widow. If a widow has no such advisors already in place, she should move slowly. Get some recommendations from friends, relatives, and professionals; then conduct personal interviews before picking an advisor who seems reliable.

A capable investment advisor can make a widow feel more comfortable. Take the case of Carol Young, whose late husband Dan had handled the couple's investments by himself. He kept most of their portfolio in a junk bond fund.

At Dan's death, Carol was only 68. She needed growth and inflation protection in her portfolio, considering her good health and long life expectancy. Moreover, trusting her future to junk bonds seemed much too risky.

Her investment advisor explained to Carol why she should diversify among various types of investments. Carol consented so most of the shares in the junk bond fund were sold and the sales proceeds were reinvested.

Some of that money was moved into stock funds, for growth, and her bond portfolio was upgraded to Treasuries and high-quality corporate bonds. Those bonds provide enough current income to maintain Carol's lifestyle (a key concern of hers) while the stocks are likely to offer some appreciation and inflation protection.

NEVER TOO LATE TO LEARN

Again, relying upon knowledgeable advisors is fine but education is vital for widows. Through reading and discussions with financial advisors, widows can learn some important concepts: the various types of investment risk, current income versus total return, and how holding down risks likely will lead to lower returns.

Women tend to invest more conservatively than men. For a widow, that's probably just as well because an emphasis on income-producing bonds and bond funds may be appropriate. Widows may feel comfortable if they hold ample liquid assets, so speculative securities might be sold and the proceeds held in cash equivalents.

Widows may not think they need growth but they shouldn't overdose on cash and bonds. Some equities are necessary for inflation protection. Even the oldest investors would likely do well with at least 20% of a portfolio in stocks. Dividend-paying stocks can provide both current income and growth potential; under the current tax law, income from dividends will be lightly taxed.

Widows with portfolios well into six figures can hire a money manager to choose individual securities that are suitable for their needs. With smaller portfolios, widows probably would do better holding mutual funds, spreading the wealth among many issues. Most funds have modest minimum investment requirements.

HOME RUN

Beyond portfolio management, other concerns may affect a widow's finances. For example, widows often move to be close to other family members. The downside: a widow may go to the trouble and expense of relocating only to have a grown child get transferred and move across the country. To prevent such occurrences, widows might stay put and use the money they'll save to buy airplane tickets to visit their family for holidays.

Frequently, widows are comfortable in the family home and, if the mortgage has been paid off, they find they can afford to maintain it. Indeed, many widows want to keep their house because it's a source of stability. However, in many cases a single-family home is too much for one person to maintain. Within two or three years most widows will move to something simpler in terms of maintenance.

RE-LEARNING THE A-B-Cs

Such moves are often dictated by a widow's health, which is another area of prime concern. One widow's husband had been covered by retiree health care benefits, from his former employer. The widow could have relied upon his coverage but she decided against doing so. Instead, she enrolled in Medicare and bought a Medicare supplement (Medigap) insurance policy.

Her husband's coverage was based on a local HMO which might have created problems for her, because she travels a good deal. Outside of the HMO's area, only emergency care is covered, and claims may be questioned on the ground that no real emergency was involved. Medigap gives her more flexibility.

Often, the selection depends on where the widow lives and which companies are offering which plans. If cost is not a concern, some financial planners suggest Plan F, which will cover medical charges in excess of the amount allowed by Medicare. In the plans covering prescription drugs, the benefits might not be worth the costs.

If a widow has cost concerns, though, Plan A probably will be sufficient. Plan A covers what might be called basic exposure: hospital co-payments and doctor's bills up to Medicare-approved limits. The costs for Plan A are the lowest among Medigap policies. According to Weiss Ratings, a 65-year-old female could pay as little as $425 a year for Plan A in Utah and West Virginia, in 2004. Even in the most expensive state, New Jersey, Plan A was available for nearly $1000 per year. Other Medigap plans may cost $3,000 per year, or more.

No matter which plan is chosen, timing can be critical. If you sign up within six months of enrolling in Medicare Part B, which is medical insurance, you can't be refused Medigap coverage, even with pre-existing health problems. Anyone who waits may face restrictions. Widows who hesitate may have lost the opportunity to buy the right policy at the right price, or to buy any policy at all. Education, and the planning that results, can avoid such costly errors.

Chapter 10
Out Of Wedlock (And Back In Again)

Life's ups and downs can complicate estate planning. After a divorce, for example, new plans are vital. Moreover, many divorcees and widows or widowers remarry, which leads to yet another set of concerns.

When it comes to divorce, the key for both parties is to preserve as much of their estate (their assets) as possible. Perhaps the best tactic is to cut back on the use of lawyers. In major metro areas, divorce lawyers charge \$250-\$500 per hour. Divorces mean two law firms on the clock, so the hourly fees can reach \$1,000 per hour.

Every thousand dollars billed by the lawyers is a thousand dollars the couple won't have to divide. Increasingly, divorcing couples use mediation, where reliance on lawyers is minimized or eliminated. If that's not feasible, the parties should try to reach a mutual settlement as quickly as possible, cutting down on lawyers' bills.

To get a fair settlement in a divorce, all assets should be disclosed and appropriately valued. In community property states (including California, Texas, and Arizona), each spouse is entitled to 50% of the assets accrued during the marriage. The other states tend to follow the rule of "equitable distribution," which essentially means that it's up to a judge to decide what's evenhanded. The more accurate the couple's financial statements, the more likely both sides will get a reasonable deal.

Generally, property settlements begin with a "yours, mine, and ours" approach. Property that each spouse brought into the marriage, and kept in a separate name, has a good chance of remaining with that spouse. The same is true of property acquired during the marriage. If Jack inherited 100 shares of GE from Aunt Jane before or while he was married to Jill and kept them in his own name, there's often no reason that Jill should be entitled to Jack's GE shares. On the other hand, if Jack swept those shares into their joint brokerage account, then they likely will be considered marital property, subject to a property division.

KEEPING COMPANY

There are some exceptions to this practice. If a valid prenuptial agreement is in place, it may control the property division. Although not every prenup holds up, an agreement in which each spouse was represented by independent, competent attorneys probably will be sustained, especially if there are no assertions of coercion or inadequate financial disclosure.

A more complicated situation may arise when one spouse's premarital assets include a closely-held company. Suppose Jack went into the marriage holding all the shares of ABC Software, a startup business with little apparent value. Over the years, Jack has built ABC Software into a thriving enterprise, valued at $2 million.

Jack may still hold all the shares but Jill no doubt will contend that Jack's success was due in large part to her running the household, raising the kids, and relieving Jack of other responsibilities so that he could concentrate on software. She'll want to share in that growth, and may well be entitled to a substantial portion—even half—of its worth.

As a practical matter, though, Jack probably will not want his ex-spouse holding 50% (or even 5%) of his business. If Jack has one or more co-shareholders, those shareholders may be even less enthused about welcoming Jill into their ranks. In many circumstances, a buy-sell agreement will be in place, giving the co-shareholders or Jack himself the obligation to keep shares from an ex-spouse. Indeed, if

Jack had previously transferred shares in ABC Software to Jill, the buy-sell may call for those shares to be acquired.

If the buyout is to be in cash, some complications can be avoided. The main concern will be to make certain that the business is properly valued. Each spouse may want to hire his or her own appraiser. If the stakes are large enough, the non-owner spouse might bring in a "forensic accountant," who doubles as a detective on the track of hidden assets. (Indeed, forensic accountants may be a good idea in any divorce where one spouse suspects the other is not disclosing everything.)

In many cases, though, owners of small companies won't have a great deal of cash on hand, so the non-owner spouse will have to settle for other assets, such as securities, or a promissory note. If a note is involved, the spouse on the receiving end should be sure the note is well collateralized with assets outside of the business, such as a house. That spouse should do a title search to make sure the same asset isn't being used as collateral for other lines of credit: no one wants to be in line behind a bank if an ex-spouse defaults on a note.

MAKING DIVORCE LESS TAXING

The IRS expects all property issues in a divorce to be settled within two years, so the recipient should try not to stretch out a note longer than that—subsequent payments may be considered part taxable income, rather than a tax-free property settlement. If the two-year limit isn't feasible, the spouse receiving the payments may want to ask for a short-term and a long-term note, front-loading as much as possible into the first note.

If securities are given instead of cash, basis becomes a critical concern. Indeed, basis is important whenever appreciated assets are included in a divorce settlement—a point that's ignored by many divorce lawyers.

Suppose, for example, that Jill agrees to accept $200,000 in securities in return for allowing Jack to keep all shares in ABC Software.

Jack owns $200,000 worth of X mutual fund and $200,000 worth of Y mutual fund in his own account, dating back to the days before their marriage. How can Jill decide which fund to accept?

Actually, neither holding will bring complete satisfaction. Suppose Jack's basis in fund X is $50,000. After a transfer pursuant to a divorce settlement, Jill will have Jack's basis. If she sells all the shares, she'll have a $150,000 gain and owe about $22,500 in tax, assuming a 15% capital gains tax rate. So this $200,000 "asset" is really worth about $177,500 to her. If Jack's holdings in fund Y have a $100,000 basis, those shares would be worth around $185,000 to Jill, after tax.

Jack might counter that his interest in ABC Software is worth less than face value because he'll owe capital gains tax if he sells.

That's true, but Jack may hold onto those shares indefinitely, perhaps passing them down to his children at his death with a step-up in basis. These factors should all be brought out and assets should be divided on an after-tax rather than a pre-tax basis.

UP WITH ALIMONY

Taxes also should play a role in shaping the overall divorce settlement. By emphasizing alimony, which is tax-deductible, rather than child support or a property settlement, which aren't, both sides may wind up winning.

Suppose Jack proposes to pay $2,000 per month in child support. He'd be out of pocket the $2,000 and Jill would receive $2,000 each month. Instead, Jack, who has an effective income tax rate of 40%, might pay $2,500 in alimony each month to Jill, who's in a 15% bracket.

With the latter approach, Jack saves $1,000 in taxes each month (40% of $2,500), bringing his net cost down to $1,500. Jill will owe $375 per month in taxes (15% of $2,500), but she'll still net $2,125 and have more money to spend.

Naturally, the IRS knows how this game is played so it looks hard to see whether alimony is child support or a property settlement in disguise. That's why it's vital that all the rules regarding alimony are followed. For example, the payments must end at the recipient's death.

In real life, the issue of alimony-versus -child support-versus-property settlement won't prove to be as simple as this Jack-and-Jill example. However, the tax law favors alimony when there's a wide difference between the parties' tax brackets, so it's generally advisable for the divorce agreement to include alimony to the greatest extent possible.

MAXIMUM SECURITY

Besides taxes, another issue that's sometimes overlooked in divorce negotiations is Social Security benefits. (Don't belittle Social Security: annual retirement benefits in 2003 may be greater than $2,000 per month, over $25,000 per year. That's more income than someone would receive from $800,000 in the bank, paying 3% interest. Moreover, Social Security benefits are indexed to inflation.) Divorced spouses are eligible for spousal and widow's benefits—in some cases, the terms are even better for divorced spouses—as long as the marriage lasted at least 10 years.

If the higher-earning spouse remarries, the divorced spouse's benefits won't be affected. The divorced spouse will be entitled to either spousal benefits or widow's benefits as long as she doesn't remarry before age 60.

Therefore, it doesn't make sense to have a divorce decree finalized 9-1/2 years into a marriage. The parties should try to reach the 10-year mark before making the divorce official. Assuming the marriage has lasted 10 years and the lower-earning spouse will be eligible for increased Social Security benefits, the higher-earning spouse should factor that increase into the total settlement, reducing the amount of other assets he'll have to part with. In addition, federal law permits a tax-deferred retirement account and a pension plan to be split in a divorce settlement without accelerating income tax.

SPLIT WITHOUT GETTING FRACTURED

After a divorce, tax savings can help the former spouses build their estates. In many cases, a taxpayer's bill will be lower if he or she files as a "head of household," rather than as a single person or as "married, filing separately."

For example, under the 2003 tax act, the 15% bracket covers up to $28,400 in taxable income for single filers and for married people filing separately that year. Heads of household have a 15% bracket all the way up to $38,050 in taxable income. After those thresholds, the tax rate jumps to 25%.

It's true that the tax rates on a joint return are even more favorable but spouses might not want to file jointly if a marriage is ending. If the IRS audits a joint return and finds a shortfall, it can dun either spouse for the entire amount of additional taxes, interest, and penalties.

Regardless of whether someone is divorced or even legally separated, it's still possible to qualify for favorable head-of-household tax rates by meeting these tests:

1. The taxpayer files a separate return from the spouse or ex-spouse.
2. The couple never lived together during the last six months of the year.
3. The taxpayer paid over half the household's costs during the year.
4. For over half the year, the taxpayer's home was the principal residence of a dependent child.

If one spouse can't claim the child as a dependent, that spouse still can be a head-of-household if the dependency exemption was signed over to the other spouse that year on IRS Form 8332.

KID STUFF

Dependency exemptions are valuable tax breaks. In 2004, taxpayers can deduct $3,500 for each dependent.

Who gets to claim the kids as dependents, after a separation or divorce? The dependency exemptions usually go to the custodial parent, as specified in a divorce or separation agreement. Without such an agreement, the parent with physical custody for most of the year gets the tax break.

However, some custodial parents have little or no taxable income. If so, the dependency exemptions are worth little or nothing, in terms of tax relief.

To maximize the tax savings, a low-income custodial parent can sign over the dependency exemptions to the higher-income parent, on IRS Form 8332. To the higher-income parent, these exemptions may result in greater tax savings. In a 40% effective tax bracket, for example, each $3,050 exemption saves over $1,200 in federal income tax. Generally, the custodial spouse receives some concession in the separation or divorce negotiations, in return for agreeing to sign Form 8332.

Negotiating strategies:

- For the custodial spouse. The best approach is to sign away dependency exemptions on a yearly basis, rather than grant an indefinite waiver. Signing the waiver each year can help to assure that the ex-spouse will comply with child support and alimony obligations.
- For the non-custodial spouse. Be careful about making concessions in return for the dependency exemptions if your adjusted gross income (AGI) is over certain levels. A phase-out reduces the benefits of all dependency exemptions claimed by high-income taxpayers. In 2003, for example, the phase-out begins at $139,500 for single filers. Once a single filer's AGI tops $262,000, dependency exemptions provide no tax benefit.

Similarly, the dependency exemption does not help taxpayers who are subject to the alternative minimum tax (AMT). Thus, it doesn't make sense to offer negotiating concessions in return for dependency exemptions if you expect to pay the AMT.

THE SECOND TIME AROUND

Just as many marriages end in divorce, so many once-wed individuals are willing to try again (and perhaps again). In the event of a remarriage, estate planning can be vital to all the parties involved.

If you have children from a previous marriage, you should take steps to protect them, especially if those children are young. It's not realistic to expect a new spouse to have the same loyalties to those children as your former spouse.

However, when some people remarry they put all of their assets in joint name with the new spouse or they make wills leaving everything to that spouse. There may be a verbal agreement that the new spouse "will take care of the children" if anything should happen, but that puts the children from the first marriage at risk.

PRENUP POWER

Although the idea may seem materialistic, a well-executed prenuptial agreement removes a large area of uncertainty and puts everyone's mind at ease. As long as a prenup is structured fairly, a source of potential friction is removed.

Terms of a prenup will vary, according to the circumstances, but the basic structure is yours-mine-ours. That is, each spouse will retain the assets he or she brings into the marriage while assets accumulated during the marriage will be owned by both. Prenuptial agreements need to anticipate death as well as divorce, so the same principles can be extended to an estate plan within the agreement. The amount of net worth you accumulate before your second marriage might go to the children from your first marriage while assets accumulated subsequently might go to your second spouse and any children from that marriage. You should try to keep things equitable, without penalizing anyone.

A prenup can cover everything from household spending to disposition of assets in case of death or divorce. In some states, a surviving spouse is automatically entitled to a certain share in the other spouse's estate but such an entitlement can be waived through a valid prenup.

When a couple is planning on remarrying, talking about a prenuptial agreement can be awkward, to say the least. A reluctance to enter into a prenup is understandable: people want to be in a strong relationship with a trusted party, and to demonstrate this trust they may share all of their assets with the new spouse. But that's not fair to the children of the first marriage, especially if there eventually are children from the remarriage.

Fair or not, asking a spouse-to-be to provide a list of assets for a prenup isn't going to win you any points at home. One tactic is to tell your prospective spouse that you're revising your entire estate plan–which you should be doing. That estate plan might include a prenup along with a new will, trusts, etc.

Another approach is to tell your spouse is that you have an advisor, such as an accountant or attorney or financial planner, who insists that you have a prenup agreement in place before taking new vows. Blame anyone you want, but just make sure you get a prenup in place.

To overcome prenup discomfort, you may want to downplay the possibility of divorce. Instead, you might focus on what will happen when one spouse dies. Both spouses will want their own children to be protected, so there may be more acceptance of the idea of a prenuptial agreement.

COME TOGETHER

A prenuptial agreement should be coordinated with your will, any trust documents, and other elements of your estate plan. You don't want your will to leave certain assets to your children while those same assets are given to your new spouse as part of a prenuptial agreement.

Whether or not you have a prenuptial agreement, anyone who brings assets into a remarriage and has concerns about the disposition of those assets should have a will. What's more, your will should be prepared by an attorney who specializes in estate planning.

In a remarriage, estate planning can be a particularly thorny issue. One spouse may be worried about dying and leaving assets to the other spouse. That spouse may then leave all of those assets to his or her own children, shutting out the children of the first spouse to die, the one who provided the assets.

In such circumstances, you might use a trust. The spouse who sets up the trust names the trustee, generally someone from his or her own side of the family. The trustee is instructed to provide the surviving spouse with the amounts necessary for health, education, maintenance, and support. At some point, perhaps when the decedent's own children turn 30 or 35, the trustee can distribute trust assets to them.

But not all estate plans work out so easily. Jean Williams, for example, has a large income and substantial assets, with two grown sons who are doing well. Her husband George isn't working and his five kids haven't accomplished much in life. When they sat down to come up with an estate plan, George said all of the couple's assets should be divided 50-50 but Jean wouldn't agree to that.

They resolved this dispute by buying a second-to-die life insurance policy that would pay off after both of their deaths. George's children would be the beneficiaries and collect the proceeds, tax-free, while Jean's children would get her assets.

THE QTIP FLIP

Another useful technique in estate planning for remarried couples is the use of a "QTIP" (Qualified Terminable Interest Property) trust. Assets left to such a trust are considered marital assets so no estate tax is due at the first spouse's death. All income from the trust goes to the surviving spouse. Sometimes, but not always, the survivor will have access to the trust principal, too.

After the death of the surviving spouse, estate tax will be due and the remaining trust assets will go to heirs named by the trust creator. Thus, you can direct the assets to the children of your first marriage, if that's your desire.

It can be very difficult for the surviving spouse to understand that she has no control over the ultimate disposition of the trust assets so a certain amount of explaining usually is required. Nevertheless, a QTIP can be a valuable tool–you might, for example, name a QTIP trust as retirement plan beneficiary. If the remarriage ends in a divorce, you can change the beneficiary designation back to your grown children, so there is some room to adapt to changing circumstances.

QTIP trusts pose additional estate planning challenges, though. They're extremely complicated so you should work with an attorney who specializes in estate planning. Technical shortcomings may lead to an estate tax obligation at the first rather than the second spouse's death.

TROUBLE FOR THE TRUSTEE

What's more, QTIP trusts may put the trustee in an awkward position, having to decide between the interests of the surviving spouse and those of the ultimate beneficiaries. In some cases, the surviving spouse wants everything in bonds, even risky high-yield bonds, to maximize annual income, and won't care if the principal is stable or shrinks a bit. The children from the first marriage, on the other hand, may be urging the trustee to invest in growth stocks so their inheritance will appreciate, even if there is scant income for the surviving spouse.

A viable plan in such cases might be the use of a "total return" rather than a "current income" approach: invest largely in stocks and sell some each year to provide adequate cash flow to the surviving spouse. Such a strategy appealed to Al Collins, a retiree who was remarried, with children from his first marriage.

There was no prenuptial agreement so Al had to work out an estate plan that would provide for all parties yet avoid the threat of his wife electing against his will. If he did what might be considered normal—creating a trust that will pay income to his surviving spouse—she might be unhappy with a payout of around 2%.

Such a problem suggested the adoption of a total return uni-trust. This trust will pay Al's surviving spouse 4% per year. That would double her income, vs. 2% from a pay-income trust, so she might agree not to contest the will. Such an agreement may get the trustee out of the middle and reduce the risk that the whole arrangement will be blown up, after Al's death.

The competing desires of a surviving spouse and children from a prior marriage are especially difficult to balance when interest income and dividend yields are at current low levels. With a total return trust, though, all parties' interests may be served.

For example, suppose a trust pays 4% to the income beneficiary in Year One and the trust principal grows by 8% that year. The income beneficiary will receive 4% of a larger principal amount in Year Two, collecting a larger check, while the remainder beneficiaries will see their stake grow. A typical uni-trust will pay out 3%, 4%, or 5% a year, while the trustee has the discretion to pay more, if necessary.

Often, a family member will serve as co-trustee with a corporate trustee, which provides long-term stability. Generally, payouts are based on a percentage of assets; using a three-year rolling average can smooth out year-to-year fluctuations in distributions.

In some total return trusts, distribution arrangements move away from straight percentage payouts to give some flexibility to the trustee or to automatically increase the percentage as young beneficiaries grow older. An alternative is to use a traditional pay-income trust that gives the income beneficiary the right to demand up to, say, 5% of the trust principal each year. Such provisions effectively give the income beneficiary the ability to transform a pay-income trust to a total return trust.

Yet another problem relates to the timing of QTIP distributions. Suppose a husband dies at age 80, leaving a 60-year-old widow and children from a first marriage who are 55 and 50. By the time his widow dies and his children inherit, they could be well into their 70s, having spent the past 20 years waiting for their stepmother to die so they can inherit—if there is anything left to inherit.

Liquidity may be a concern, too, especially for people who accumulate most of their wealth in a tax-deferred retirement plan. Such a plan, held in a QTIP trust, can pass from surviving spouse to the children of a first marriage. However, estate tax may be due then. If the estate tax needs to be paid from the IRA, withdrawals will trigger income tax as well, stripping out a great deal of the plan's value and sharply reducing the children's inheritance.

LETTING GO

What techniques can be used to avoid such problems? If you feel that you have more than enough wealth to provide comfortably for yourself and your spouse, you might give away some of that wealth to your children while you're still alive.

In 2004, you can give up to $11,000 worth of assets ($22,000 if your spouse consents) to any number of recipients each year, free of gift tax. Those limits are indexed to inflation in $1,000 increments, so you'll likely be able to give away up to $12,000 or $24,000 per recipient per year, starting in 2004 or 2005. (In addition, you can make direct payments of a grandchild's tuition expense without any gift tax consequences.)

Whether or not you make lifetime gifts, you can make outright bequests to your children at your death. In 2004, you can leave up to $1.5 million worth of assets to your children, free of federal estate tax, a number that will increase to $3.5 million by 2009. Thus, it's possible to leave some assets to your children from a first marriage and some assets, outright or in trust, to a second spouse.

If you choose this strategy, you need to decide which assets you should leave to your children. One approach is to divide your IRA into two or more IRAs. One IRA can have your spouse as beneficiary while the other IRA or IRAs can be left to each of your children. You determine how much goes into each IRA. It's a relatively easy process and it provides each heir with control over an IRA.

Another option is to keep your IRA intact, going to your surviving spouse, while appreciated securities or real estate is left to the children. Inherited assets get a "step-up in basis," so your children can sell those assets without owing any tax on the appreciation during your lifetime. You should look at all the variables, meet with your advisers, and decide which strategy to implement.

MONETARY POLICY

Sometimes, life insurance is a vital ingredient in these strategies. You might plan on leaving the bulk of your estate to your spouse, particularly if there's a second set of children, and provide for the children from your first marriage with an insurance policy that pays off at your death. Alternatively, assets you accumulated before your second marriage can go to the children of your first marriage while life insurance protects your second spouse and her children, if any.

Insurance on your life can provide for your children from the first marriage while a 'second-to-die' policy covering both spouses can protect any children from the second marriage. If the second marriage ends in divorce you can keep the policies in force to provide for younger children. When you're planning for a remarriage you need to anticipate all contingencies and build in as much flexibility as possible.

WIN WITH WEALTH TRUSTS

To see how a sophisticated estate plan might take effect in a remarriage, consider the example of Jane and John Johnson, who are 52 and 57, respectively. Both have children and grandchildren from a previous marriage. Their total estate (IRAs, real estate, stocks, business interests) adds up to around $6 million.

What kind of planning should this remarried couple consider?

- A Revocable Living Trust. If John should become incompetent, assets held in trust can be managed by Jane, as successor trustee. No guardianship hearing will be required and intra-family feuding can be avoided.

  At John's death, the trust assets will be distributed, as per the trust documents that were created at John's direction. Those assets won't be subject to the time and expense of probate.

- Beneficiary Designation. John's IRA won't be held in the living trust so beneficiary designations are crucial. John might specify that half of his IRA will go to Jane, who can roll it over into her own IRA. The other half of John's IRA might be divided among John's children, who can stretch out tax-deferral over their life expectancies, if they wish.

- The Wealth Trust® #1 (personal access version). Jane can establish a Personal Access Wealth Trust for John's children. First, John could transfer $1 million of his personal assets to Jane, as her own separate property. Then, Jane could give $1 million to the Personal Access Wealth Trust, using her $1 million gift-tax exemption. John can be both the trustee and a beneficiary of this trust, assuming that it's drafted properly. Thus, he can tap the trust fund if an emergency arises.

  At John's death, this trust can divide into subtrusts, one for each of John's children, who will have access to the funds in his or her subtrust. No estate tax will be due at this time because the assets won't be in John's estate. The assets in these subtrusts will be protected from creditors, lawsuits, and divorcing spouses. Any assets not consumed by John's children can continue to be held in trust, estate tax-free, for the benefit of John's grandchildren.

Notice that this strategy does not diminish John's estate tax exemption. If his death occurs in 2004, for example, he can leave up to $1.5 million to his children, free of estate tax. That would be in addition to the $1 million from this Wealth Trust. If John lives for many years before his death, the $1 million in this Wealth Trust may grow to $2 million or more while even greater amounts might be left to John's children, tax-free, depending on future changes in the tax law.

- The Wealth Trust® # 2. Because Jane utilized her $1 million gift tax exemption when she transferred assets into a trust for John and his children, John will replace this amount with $1 million worth of variable universal life insurance. The policy will be held in a second Wealth Trust.

  John would fund this trust with approximately $13,500 per year over a 20-year period. If Jane lives for 20 years or more, the total cost will be $270,000 in premiums.

  On the other hand, if John retains that $270,000 in his estate, it may be worth only $148,500 to his heirs (assuming a 45% estate tax). The insurance proceeds, held in a Wealth Trust, can avoid both income and estate tax. Thus, this strategy can replace assets worth $148,500, after tax, with $1 million of after-tax dollars. That $1 million may grow in the future, tax-free, for the benefit of Jane's heirs. Thus, the asset repositioning can help all the children and grandchildren of this remarriage.

- The Wealth Trust® #3. As another part of this plan, John could establish a third Wealth Trust, of which his children are the beneficiaries. This trust might be funded initially with $500,000 of variable universal life insurance on John's life.

> Over the years, as the estate grows over $6 million, excess assets can be given to this Wealth Trust and used to pay the life insurance premiums. Savvy estate planning professionals can use the annual gift-tax exclusion and so-called Crummey notices to avoid any gift-tax obligation from these transfers.
>
> This strategy freezes the estate at $6 million, where the estate tax might be minimal, depending on the tax law in effect at John's and Jane's deaths. In the meantime, the money in this Wealth Trust, invested through a variable universal life policy, may grow well in excess of $500,000, to be used for covering estate tax obligations and for additional support of John's descendants.

By diversifying assets and utilizing a combination of Wealth Trusts, couples such as John and Jane Johnson may create a separate estate with the potential for enriching future generations, while reducing the potential for conflict between different groups of beneficiaries.

TRUST TACTICS

Obviously, trusts can be extremely valuable in estate planning for remarried couples. Care must be exercised, though, to resolve disagreements that may appear after one spouse's death. This real-life example shows how the trustee may face difficult alternatives:

In any marriage, including a remarriage, a spouse has certain rights to the other spouse's employer-sponsored retirement plan. Those rights don't extend to IRAs, though, so it is important to treat the beneficiary designation carefully.

State law has to be considered but one case, decided in New York, illustrates how conflicts can arise. Here, a trust was the beneficiary of the decedent's IRA. According to the trust documents, "the trustee may pay the debts of the estate."

Among the debts of the estate, substantial amounts were owed to the decedent's widow, who was the second wife. Because the estate had virtually no assets, outside of this trust, the widow asked the trust for repayment of those debts.

However, the beneficiary of the trust was the decedent's daughter from a prior marriage. Obviously, she would suffer financially if the trustee were to repay the debts by using trust assets, including the proceeds of the IRA, which were payable to the trust.

The beneficiary was a minor so the trustee asked the court for direction, as to whether debts could be paid from the trust. The verdict? Even though the trustee had the discretion to pay the debts, the court held that the trustee could not take money from the IRA to pay the creditor (the second wife) because IRAs are protected from creditors, under New York State law. Indeed, most states protect IRAs from creditors. A well-drafted trust, then, would have allowed for the repayment of this debt without burdening the trustee with making an unpleasant decision.

ALL IN THE FAMILY

As the above example indicates, remarried couples should be concerned about suits brought among family members. Especially where there's substantial net worth in a remarriage, consider suggesting a "family integrity agreement." By signing such an agreement, family members promise not to go to court in case of disputes over money. Instead, they agree to submit any arguments to binding arbitration.

Often, some family member will feel slighted over money matters. Perhaps funds have been distributed to some trust beneficiaries but not to others. By removing the threat of a lawsuit, you remove the unhappy person's trump card; they can't say, "I'll take you to court." So these agreements encourage the family members to work things out among themselves. Even if a dispute can't be resolved, binding arbitration tends to be faster and cheaper than litigation.

EYES ON THE PRIZE

In addition to the legally binding arrangements mentioned above, some informal methods may help smooth the path of a remarriage. A couple about to be remarried might sit down and talk about their goals, what they want to do with the rest of their lives. That conversation can be summarized in a memo, approved by both parties. A few years in the future, in case of problems, they can bring out that memo to see whether anything has changed. This often helps them regain sight of the big picture and pay less attention to relatively minor difficulties that have arisen.

Such strategies may help middle-aged as well as elderly remarried couples. Indeed, couples who still have children living at home are by no means immune to the stresses of remarried life.

What issues might concern blended families?

- Child support. Leftover financial rights and obligations may complicate matters. In some blended families one spouse will have to make child support payments to a former spouse. There may be income, too, if one spouse is receiving child support payments. The family's budget must be planned with these factors in mind.

  Often, there's an ex-spouse with a responsibility to make child support payments. If the custodial spouse remarries someone with substantial means, that ex-spouse might go to court to have the child support payments reduced or eliminated. That's bound to put a strain on the remarried couple. Remarrying couples should be aware that this could happen, get good counsel if necessary, and provide the emotional support that's needed.

- Home ownership. Among the most important assets to be considered, of course, is the place where you'll live: in a home that the bride or the groom already owns or in a different one?

Often, moving into a home already owned by one spouse or the other won't be ideal. A husband might feel that he's moving into his wife's home, for example, where he's just a visitor. Some advisors recommend that couples sell the house or houses they own and buy one that's really "their house," to suit the needs of the new family.

- Retirement plans. You should update your beneficiary designations. If you have life insurance and retirement plans, make sure the proceeds will go to the proper parties, after a death. You probably won't want your ex-spouse to remain the beneficiary of your IRA, for example.

  When making decisions about retirement plans, keep in mind that spouses are entitled to be the beneficiaries of employer-sponsored plans, unless those rights are waived. If you intend to designate someone besides your spouse, such as a child from a previous marriage, as a retirement plan beneficiary, be aware that a spouse's rights may only be waived by a spouse. Thus, such a waiver can't be included in a prenuptial agreement.

  However, a prenuptial agreement might include a promise that such rights will be waived after the marriage, and penalties can be established, in the prenup agreement, in case of failure to fulfill such a promise.

STRESS TEST

Handling money during a remarriage can lead to stress. Take the case of Gene and Diana Walker, a couple in their mid-40s. Diana, who has a child from a previous marriage, thinks that she should keep her assets separate, to protect her child, while Gene's assets go into the communal pot. Gene, as might be expected, is not sure this arrangement is fair.

What can be done in such a situation? If there are relatives to be protected or any other insecurities, the assets may be better off if they're kept separate. In the case of relatively young couples, time may overcome the problem. Gene and Diana, for example, have a substantial income so they can save large amounts each year. If they stay together for any length of time, their joint savings probably will far outstrip the amount that either spouse brought into the marriage, so Diana's separate holdings may become less important.

In some remarriages among relatively young spouses, the children of one spouse will still be living at home while the children of the other spouse are living independently. This can create problems if the older spouse has already paid to educate his children. Should he pay to educate his step-children, too, especially now that college costs are so great? Situations vary but step-children probably should be provided with an education because it's so important in today's world.

You may want to term in a spousal ILIT so if young spouses remarry the other heirs are not disinherited. This is sometimes called a "floating spouse" clause.

TITLE GAMES

Regardless of the ages of the remarried couple, certain financial planning questions must be answered. One issue that needs to be addressed is whether the couple's assets should be owned jointly or individually.

Holding assets in joint name with your spouse may make your home life easier but will cost you flexibility. All jointly held property will automatically go to your spouse if you're the first to die. If you transfer your brokerage account into joint name, for example, all of those securities will pass to your spouse and not to your children.

Thus, the drawback to joint ownership is that the surviving owner inherits the property, no matter what you put into your will. If you have some other intent, joint ownership won't work. The bottom line is that you need to coordinate your entire plan–your will, your property ownership, your life insurance, your trusts–to get the results you want.

Frequently, it's best for each party to preserve the assets they had going into the marriage, rather than commingle them. That will make it easier for each spouse to leave a fair portion of assets to his or her children. If assets are commingled they become marital property, weakening the claims of the children of the spouse who dies first.

Trusts are an alternative to individual ownership; the person the spouse wants to protect can be the trust beneficiary. Another approach is to use a "transfer-on-death" designation, which is available for may types of assets, including securities. Transfer-on-death assets are owned individually, not jointly. However, at the owner's death, the assets automatically go to the named beneficiary. ("TOD" ownership can be used by unmarried individuals, too, so people who are living together might consider this form of ownership.)

REAL CONCERNS

Real estate can be another complex issue. If both spouses come into the marriage with homes, which one should they live in? How should that house be titled? If one house is sold, what should happen to the sale proceeds? If taxes are owed, who'll pay them? Who'll pay the ongoing housing expenses? These are all questions that need to be answered before the marriage or shortly thereafter. A CPA might go over all the tax consequences so both spouses feel that they've come out of the negotiation with a fair deal.

Under present law, the sale of a primary residence is tax-free as long as the gain is no more than $250,000. If the seller files a joint return, the tax-free amount climbs to $500,000. Thus, if a remarrying couple plans to sell a home that will generate a gain larger than $250,000, they might want to wait until after they're married to sell that house.

While the tax expert is on hand, the couple might ask when they should remarry. A December 2004 marriage, for example, will enable them to file a joint return for 2004 while a January 2005 marriage will permit each to file singly for 2005. A tax pro can run the numbers and advise which wedding date will result in the lowest overall tax bill.

FINAL THOUGHTS

Other estate planning issues need to be settled, either before the remarriage or immediately afterwards. New wills should be executed. Trusts may be called for, depending on the situation.

If you want to establish revocable living trusts, to avoid probate and provide for incapacity, should the successor trustee be the other spouse or one of the grantor's children? Often, it's the spouse who is named as the successor, especially if the children are relatively young, and aren't ready to be named as successor trustee.

No matter how refined the estate plan, it often comes down to a choice: after the older and perhaps wealthier spouse dies, will the bulk of his assets pass to his children or to his spouse? The financial security of the surviving spouse is a concern in many remarriages, and that security often will come at the expense of the other spouse's children.

There's no simple way to handle this issue but it's generally best if the children are aware of the parents' estate plan. One tactic is to bring all the interested parties together to explain what's being done, and why. If the children live far away from their parents, they may be informed by letters or even through a conference call. There shouldn't be any surprises when the first spouse dies. At the end of the game, as well as in the beginning, careful planning may be needed to keep a blended family together.

Chapter 11
Leaving A Legacy

Chances are you expect to leave a legacy of peace and prosperity. After your death, it's likely that your heirs will inherit considerable wealth. These assets, combined with their own earnings, will probably enable them to enjoy comfortable lifestyles.

Unfortunately, the reality may be much different. In many families, there were disagreements among the children while they were growing up. When assets pass to their generation, those disputes are likely to reappear, in greater intensity. In extreme circumstances, survivors might fight over a few wooden spoons or a box of Band-Aids.

Other problems may arise after your death. If a great deal of money is involved, your heirs may fall victim to predators or spend the money foolishly. Valued property, such as real estate, may be mismanaged. In remarriage situations, there may be ill feelings between your surviving spouse and your own children.

Such complications probably can't be avoided altogether but they can be alleviated, especially if you anticipate them. The time you take to help your heirs prepare for the future can pay off in a legacy of relative harmony.

ESTATE PLANNING = INHERITANCE PLANNING = OPPORTUNITY TO PASS YOUR VALUES WITH YOUR ASSETS

To help things go smoothly after you make your final exit, give your children a reasonable idea of what they can expect to inherit.

Your children may see you enjoying a certain lifestyle in your pre-retirement and retirement years, so that's what they expect, after you're gone. In truth, taxes and debt repayment might eat up a large chunk of your wealth while dividing the balance among several siblings may reduce each one's inheritance.

Suppose, for example, that you and your spouse have accumulated $2 million, which enables you to draw down six figures a year and enjoy retirement. Each of your three children, though, can expect to inherit less than $700,000, so if they spend at the same rate the money will quickly vanish.

In such situations, a frank talk with your children may be appropriate. Go over the numbers with them–let them know they'll have to build up their own retirement fund rather than rely upon a huge inheritance.

Such straight talk may inject a dose of reality into your children's expectations and avoid conflict, but it's not likely to stamp out family squabbles after your death. In fact, arguments may become more intense if the children are desperate to get as much as possible from your estate.

OUTSIDE OVERSIGHT

One way to reduce tensions is to name an independent party as your estate's executor. A reliable professional advisor might serve, for example. If your estate plan calls for a trust to be established, name an independent trustee.

You should name several, in case one or two are unable to serve, which may happen. Your heirs are not likely to appreciate paying for an executor or trustee but, if you name a surviving relative as executor or trustee, the pressure may be enormous.

What's more, an executor assumes a fiduciary responsibility that may be better left to an outsider, or even to an institution. One of an executor's roles is to file an estate tax return, pay any estate tax due, and eventually distribute the estate's assets. What happens if the return is later audited and more estate tax is due? The executor is legally responsible and the other heirs may not be willing to give some of their money back to pay the tax. When you name an institution you shift that liability away from a family member.

Naming an independent trustee and executor can take some pressure from your heirs but how can you prepare them to handle the assets they'll inherit? Have them meet with your advisors; let them know what you're doing.

For example, they should meet with your attorney and accountant for an explanation of the tax planning strategies that you're developing, so they can be carried on after your death. If you have a broker or financial planner, your heirs should all meet with this investment advisor for some educational sessions. Otherwise, a carefully constructed portfolio of securities might be sold after your death, and then reinvested in a few highly speculative issues or even a fraudulent scheme.

PROPERTY RIGHTS

Investment property presents special problems. A securities portfolio can be divided among two or three children, but it's not so easy to divide a building. You might find your heirs unable to agree how the property should be managed or whether capital improvements should be made.

As a parent, you have to be realistic. Ask yourself whether all of your children really can manage the property as a group. Often, you're better off leaving investment property to the one child or two children who really know how to manage real estate while leaving your other heirs other assets instead. Alternatively, you might provide that your children can buy out the others, at a price set by an independent appraisal.

All of these issues should be addressed while you're alive. You might, for example, explain why John is being left an office building while Mary gets a specially designated IRA as an offset.

PARTNERSHIP PAYOFF

Ideally, a family meeting is a good place to raise such issues. In reality, though, family meetings tend to go unattended, or to degenerate into shouting matches.

As an alternative, you might create a Family Limited Partnership (FLP), then call a meeting of the partners. Such a meeting likely will be more serious and businesslike because it serves the purpose of managing valuable assets held by the family members as a united group.

Suppose, for example, you transfer your securities portfolio and investment property into an FLP. You give away limited partnership interests to your children–you can do this over a period of years to reduce gift tax consequences–while you retain control as the general partner.

Because the general partner manages all partnership assets, you still control everything in the FLP. Nevertheless, the children own valuable assets so they should be included in meetings to discuss these assets. Over the years, the children will learn by observing. They'll see how your handle your securities portfolio, perhaps, or your investment property. They'll be able to ask questions and participate in the discussions. Eventually, they'll be better able to manage those assets, after they inherit, or they'll appreciate why it makes sense to sell their share of investment property to a sibling with more real estate experience.

TIME FOR A TRUST

Even with such forethought, though, you may feel that your children aren't ready to inherit your assets. They might not have shown sufficient maturity. They might not be on a promising career path or they might have shown a tendency to run up debts. In some situations, they may be in a shaky marriage and you fear your legacy will be eroded by divorce negotiations.

These situations call for a trust such as The Wealth Trust® to hold your assets after your death. You can place whatever restrictions you think are appropriate on the trust funds. The beneficiaries might be restricted to distributions of trust income over their lifetimes. Alternatively, some of the principal might be distributed when the beneficiaries reach a certain age, some more of the principal five or 10 years later, and so on, in hopes that the trust beneficiaries will become more capable of handling money as they grow older.

Again, it's often best to discuss the terms of a trust with the beneficiaries while you're still alive, so they'll know what to expect. Nevertheless, some people just aren't comfortable having these sorts of discussions with their children. In that case, you might prefer to leave a letter of instruction to be read–or a video to be shown–after your death, which explains your actions.

Often, a so-called "letter of instruction" is vital in an estate plan. With such a letter you can spell out who gets what piece of furniture or which collectibles, sparing your family from corrosive arguments. However, if you do leave such a letter you should keep it in a safe place, perhaps an attorney's office, and let its presence be known to all concerned, especially your executor. If you entrust the letter to one of your heirs, it may mysteriously "disappear," leading your loved ones to some un-lovely behavior. By keeping the letter secure and updating it periodically, you can be confident your family will divide up your assets in the manner you desired.

TAKING CARE OF BUSINESS

If you own or control a closely held company, there's another aspect to leaving a legacy: succession planning. You need to take certain steps to maintain the continuity of the business. When you have a succession plan in place, you know that your business will continue, even in the event of your death, disability, or retirement. Therefore, you'll be providing for your loyal employees and their dependents. In addition, you'll be providing for your own loved ones, who will inherit either a going concern or a fair value for the business you spent so much time and effort to build.

This continuity might be maintained inside or outside of your family. If you want to pass the company to a child or children via gifts or bequests, be aware that such tactics may lead to problems. Say you have three children; one has worked hard to help build the business while the other two haven't. If the business is left equally to all three children, that wouldn't be fair to the one who has worked there. On the other hand, there might not be enough assets, outside of the business, to provide much of an inheritance for the other children. Situations like these can pull a family apart.

How can you come up with a reasonably equitable outcome? One tactic is to buy life insurance and rely upon the insurance proceeds to help to even out inheritances. If you leave your son Jim an interest in a closely held company worth $2 million, your daughter Karen might be named the beneficiary of a $2 million policy on your life.

BUILDING A BETTER BUY-SELL

If you have no heir apparent, by blood or marriage, you may be able to realize the company's value from a sale to an unrelated party. In addition to the financial motivation, you may want to keep the company going because you feel a responsibility to your employees and those employees' families.

You might agree to sell your interest in the company to partners, employees, a larger company, or even to a competitor. Regardless of the identity of the chosen successor, you should have a formal agreement rather than a handshake deal. Such a "buy-sell" agreement will spell out the terms of the buyout in case of your retirement, death, or disability. If you should die while still owning part of the company, the buyer will be required to purchase your interest from your estate, providing cash for your heirs.

If you are among two or more co-owners, a buy-sell agreement should be entered into when you first create the company.

Alternatively, a buy-sell agreement can be entered into when new co-owners join the company or as you near retirement. The agreement should identify the seller, the buyer, the trigger events, and the terms of the sale.

What's more, a valid buy-sell can fix the value of your company for tax purposes. According to the tax code, a buy-sell must be bona fide, not a device to transfer the business at less than full value, and comparable to similar arrangements entered into at arm's length.

If you follow these guidelines in your buy-sell, your valuation probably will be accepted for estate tax purposes, saving your heirs an expensive fight with the IRS.

In addition, a buy-sell agreement will determine how much the buyers will have to pay in the event of your death or disability. The agreement should contain a price for your interest in the company. Make sure the value will remain current until the buy-sell takes effect.

Suppose, for example, you and a colleague are equal partners. You agree that the business is valued at $3 million so each partner's interest is worth $1.5 million. Every year you can renegotiate a new value and modify the buy-sell agreement accordingly. If one partner dies, the survivor will buy the decedent's interest at the agreed-upon price.

As another approach, you and your partner could create a mechanism for determining future value. The valuation might be based on current book value or book value without goodwill or some other measurement. The method of valuation should be examined periodically, especially if your company is growing and the ownership structure is changing.

Professionals advise bringing in an independent appraiser familiar with your industry to arrive at a valuation, then keeping that valuation up-to-date. As a bonus, a buy-sell agreement negotiated between you and unrelated co-owners provide a valuation you can rely upon for gift and estate tax purposes.

FLEX PLAN

In addition to making sure that your buy-sell agreement sets a fair purchase price, you need to decide which buyout method you want to use. With the "redemption" method, the company acquires the interest of the departed owner.

Suppose your company has four equal partners and one of your fellow owners dies. With the redemption method, the company itself buys the decedent's interest so the remaining three partners each own a one-third interest, up from one-fourth before the transaction. If you decide another partner is needed your company can offer the newcomer a full share in the business, offer a smaller share, or hire an employee.

The other type of buy-sell transaction is a "cross-purchase" agreement. The remaining partners do the acquiring. In the above example, each of the three remaining partners would buy a portion of the decedent's interest, raising their stake from one-fourth to one-third of the business.

Redemption agreements are likely to be simpler, especially if there are several partners with varying interests in the company. However, cross-purchase agreements may offer tax advantages. The remaining owners get a "basis step-up" for their acquired interests, which will reduce the tax they owe on future sales, perhaps at their own retirement. What's more, there is no chance of the IRS trying to impose "constructive dividends" (ordinary income to the recipient, non-deductible for the company), as there may be with a redemption.

When you draft a buy-sell agreement, keep the tax consequences in mind. That is, you might want to structure your buy-sell so that either your company or the other owners can buy your stock. This means that neither party has an unconditional obligation, nor no "constructive dividend" will be assessed by the IRS.

Many buy-sells are structured as cross-purchase agreements, with each principal unconditionally required to buy the other's stock, at death, retirement, disability, or even just departure from the company. Sometimes, though, the remaining principals don't have enough cash for the buyout. Then, a redemption plan might be used, with the company (now controlled by the remaining principals) buying in the shares. That's a tax trap.

The remaining principals will have been relieved of an obligation to personally buy the shares of the owner who died. The IRS considers this a constructive dividend and taxes it accordingly.

Suppose, for example, you and a colleague each own 50% of your business, valued at $3 million. Your partner dies and you are obligated to buy his interest. However, you don't have $1.5 million in your bank account so you direct the decedent's interest to be purchased by the company. The IRS will say that you have been relieved of a $1.5 million personal obligation and you will be taxed as if you received $1.5 million from your company as a taxable yet non-deductible dividend, then used the money to buy the decedent's interest. With a $1.5 million constructive dividend, you might owe nearly $600,000 to the IRS.

As an alternative, the buy-sell could have been drawn up so that you have the right of first refusal–but not an absolute obligation–to buy your partner's interest, and vice versa. If that right isn't exercised, the company is obligated to redeem that interest.

Then, if the time comes, you can weigh all the circumstances and see if it makes more sense to buy the decedent's shares directly, or through the company. If you decide to have the company do the buying, you can pass up your right of first refusal. The company can buy the decedent's interest, you won't have been relieved of any personal obligations, and you won't be taxed on a constructive dividend.

BUY-SELL BETWEEN TWO WEALTH TRUSTS

Yet another solution, if you wish to keep a family business in the family, is to use The Wealth Trust®. That is, The Wealth Trust® you have created can arrange to buy the shares of your family business in case of your death, disability or retirement.

As long as the buy-sell agreement is on fair terms, as defined in the tax code, the valuation will withstand any challenge.

The shares can be passed on to future generations, free of estate tax, while management of the company can remain in the family, under terms set by The Wealth Trust® documents.

INSURING YOUR LEGACY

Once all of the basic elements are in place, you should focus on a method for funding a buy-sell agreement. After all, there has to be an adequate pool of liquid assets to buy out your interest in case of your death.

Most buy-sells are funded, at least in part, by life insurance. If you own a $1.5 million policy on the life of a co-owner who dies, you'll collect the proceeds, free of tax, and have the money to buy the decedent's interest from his estate.

At the same time, your partner will hold a policy on your life. (The policies might be held in a trust to guard against skipped payments or policy loans.) That's another way of making sure the money will be there if and when your family needs it.

EASING THE WAY

Anyone who owns property may have yet another opportunity to leave a legacy: you can make sure that property will remain undeveloped, in perpetuity. Moreover, you may enjoy significant income tax as well as estate tax benefits. Property taxes may be lower, too.

To enjoy these tax benefits, you can donate a conservation easement to a local government or a qualified not-for-profit conservation group. This easement will permanently restrict future development on the property.

You must have development rights or other conservation-oriented rights (such as preservation of wildlife habitat) to give away. Such rights must be substantial enough so that a qualified recipient will accept the easement and agree to monitor the restriction.

Suppose you own a 100-acre parcel of land 25 miles from a major city, in the path of development. You agree to donate an easement that would prohibit commercial or industrial development while restricting residential use. (In some cases, conservation easements permit limited development.)

To get an income tax deduction, you need before-and-after appraisals of your property. Say your 50-acre property is appraised at $1 million before donating your easement. Afterwards, the value is set at $800,000. Both appraisals come from an unrelated party with an excellent reputation.

In this example, the $200,000 loss of value can be taken as a charitable deduction. Such charitable contribution deductions usually are limited to 30% of your adjusted gross income, with the excess carried forward up to five years. Thus, if you donate a large easement but have a moderate income, some of your deduction is likely to remain unused.

Alternatively, you can start with a small easement and move on to a larger one later. Take all the relief afforded by the first easement, and then begin the six-year cycle again. That approach has been upheld by the Tax Court in the Strasburg case (79 T.C.M., CCH 1697, 2000).

SHRINKING TARGET

By reducing your property's appraised value, as described above, you may be able to reduce your property tax obligation. In addition, you'll get the value of the easement out of your taxable estate.

In addition, a further estate tax exclusion is in the Internal Revenue Code. Formerly, this exclusion was limited to properties that met certain location (within 25 miles of a metro area, national park, or wilderness area) and ownership (three years prior to death) requirements.

The 2001 tax act, though, eliminated the location requirements. Now, all U.S. properties may be eligible for this estate tax exclusion, if a conservation easement is donated.

The federal estate tax exclusion is worth up to 40% of the value of the land (not structures) subject to a donated conservation easement. Suppose you grant a conservation easement, reducing the value of your property from $2 million to $1.1 million. Your house on the property is valued at $100,000.

Thus, the land subject to the easement is worth $1 million: $1.1 million minus $100,000. The 40% exclusion would reduce your taxable estate by $400,000. (The maximum exclusion is $500,000.)

However, the value of any retained development rights reduces the value of the land eligible for the exclusion. Suppose, in the above example, you had retained partial development rights worth $200,000. That would have been subtracted from the $1 million land value to get $800,000; the 40% estate tax exclusion would be worth $320,000.

To get the full 40% exclusion, an easement must reduce property value by at least 30%. Smaller easements rate a smaller deduction. A 20% reduction in property value, for example, would earn a 20% estate tax exclusion, not 40%.

If you do not grant a conservation easement during your lifetime, your executor can do so after your death, to get the estate tax exclusion. However, if you don't make a lifetime donation, you won't enjoy the income tax and property tax reductions. Estate tax benefits may be greater with a lifetime donation because of how the exclusion is calculated.

In addition, unless you donate the easement yourself you can't be sure of what will happen to the land. Therefore, if you choose not to grant an easement during your lifetime, your estate planning documents should spell out whether or not your executor has the authority to grant post-mortem easements and, if so, whether your heirs' consent is needed.

PRIVATE PROPERTY

If you decide to donate a conservation easement, you usually will not have to allow public access to your property. You'll retain title to the property and the ability to dispose of it as you wish. If you've been operating the property as a farm or ranch, that can continue.

On the other hand, donating a conservation easement probably means a true loss of resale value. Even if you never plan to sell the property, your heirs will likely receive a lower price, if they sell after your death. As mentioned, conservation easements are donated in perpetuity so they never expire.

Moreover, when you donate a conservation easement you'll incur various fees. You'll likely have to hire an appraiser, an engineer, a surveyor, an attorney, a title search expert, and probably a tax professional. Altogether, you can expect to pay a hefty total in fees so you should be sure that the tax benefits are worth the outlays.

Also, you should have a genuine interest in restricting future property development and preserving open space. Otherwise, your tax benefits may not be sustained.

For information on groups that will accept conservation easements, call the Land Trust Alliance, (202-638-4725), the Nature Conservancy (800-628-6860), or the Trust for Public Land (415-495-4014).

The bottom line is that there are many strategies you can employ in order to leave a legacy that will benefit your loved ones, your favorite causes, and society in general. The more planning you do, the greater the chance that you'll leave a legacy of which you can be proud.

Chapter 12

Unique Plans for Unique Families: Actual Case Studies

Back in 1997, I was working with a couple that had recently located to Florida from the Northeast. In going through the background process it was brought to my attention that they owned a wonderful home on a lake in New Hampshire. It was obvious from speaking with the clients that this place was special to them and was the source of a number of fond memories. On my first visit there, I was awed by the pristine beauty. Over a martini, I heard stories of children attending summer camp, weekend getaways and holidays with friends. It quickly became very clear to me that this property had much more than tangible value to this family. It wasn't so much what they said about the property, but how it was said that gave me this feeling.

As I was preparing a comprehensive plan factoring all of the objectives of the clients, we created a program that provided estate tax reduction strategies as well as wealth protection techniques for children and grandchildren. Because all of the adult children of these clients are financially independent and all but one is married, the primary plan focused on utilizing two multi-generation Wealth Trusts to provide access to assets to the children with any unused amounts passing to the grandchildren.

Once we had the core of the estate plan completed, and we created a comfortable process, I had a basic understanding of what they wanted to accomplish, and as such I would suggest ideas. They would consider the ideas and we discussed practical implementation. An interesting thing happened when we came to discuss the lake house. The rest of the plan had a general theme of providing access to assets for children with the balance protected in trust so that each child may appoint his or her share to the grandchildren or other relatives at their discretion.

Given the sentimental nature of the lake house I thought that planning for this asset would follow suit. Instead, however, the clients said something that was unexpected, at least to me. The statement was, " I would rather leave the home to the four kids because they are the ones that will have the memory of it and it will be much more meaningful to them than to the grandchildren." As such, we looked at a strategy that would provide a benefit for the children rather than multiple generations.

The objective was for the client to attain the ability to use the home during the summer for the next fifteen to twenty years, with the idea that at some point they would probably stop coming north for the summer and the children and the children's families would enjoy the lake house as a 'getaway.' Given their objectives, I considered how to best protect this asset.

The property is large, has lake frontage, and is clearly one of the best properties on the lake. I subscribe to the "old dock theory" which basically means that if you want to find the best piece of property in a given location look for the oldest dock. The theory is that the first person that is at a given location had his choice of location. Where he chose to put his dock is probably a good indication of what is the best locale.

We decided to use a Qualified Personal Residence Trust to pass the lake house to the children. A Qualified Personal Residence Trust is a trust that has two beneficiaries. There is a beneficiary for a specified term of years and a remainder beneficiary. When the trust is formed there is an irrevocable transfer to fund the trust of property or cash, etc. This gift is irrevocable and becomes trust property. During the term of the trust the income beneficiaries have the use and enjoyment of trust property. After the expiration of the term the property becomes vested in the persons who own the remainder. Since there is a transfer being made when the trust is funded, there is gift and thus transfer tax issues must be considered. The measure of the gift is not net asset value of the property transfer to the trust. Instead, it is the net asset value discounted to reflect the term of years until the property vests with the persons who hold the remainder interest. Once the trust is funded, so long as the trust creators outlive the term of the trust, the value of the property transferred to the trust plus any appreciation thereon is removed from the transferor's estate.

In this case, the property was appraised and valued at approximately $450,000. Based on a discount analysis, using the term of the trust and the applicable federal interest rate in effect at the time of the transaction, the value of the gift was in the mid-$200,000s. After considering the discounted value of the gift, and the fact that making this gift does not adversely affect the clients' cash flow position as most would agree that vacation homes are a money pit, the clients wholeheartedly embraced this strategy for this particular asset.

The clients felt that the property was going to appreciate in value in the future, and understood that the potential downside of predeceasing the term of the trust was mitigated from a financial perspective because The Wealth Trust,® for the benefit of their children and grandchildren had purchased life insurance coverage on the clients. If they predecease the term of the trust causing the property to be included in the taxable estate, the life insurance would simultaneously mature and provide an income and estate tax-free death benefit to the heirs.

Six years later, the property is valued in excess of $1 million and the clients continue to enjoy the use of the property. In several more years, the entire value of the property will be outside of the clients' estate, and will be vested in the hands of the children. The entire estate plan has been thoroughly discussed with each of the children and how it factors into their own estate planning.

FAMILY LIMITED PARTNERSHIPS

Consider the case of Jack and Diane Adams. They are in their mid-60s, with two children, George and Gloria.

Jack and Diane Adams create a Family Limited Partnership and transfer stocks, bonds, mutual funds, investment property, and shares in a family business into it.

Jack and Diane retain a 1% general partnership and transfer the 99% limited partnership interest to their children. Thus, 99% of the assets (and any subsequent appreciation) won't be included in the parents' taxable estate. Yet as general partners they still make all the management decisions regarding the business, the real estate, the securities, etc. The Family Limited Partnership may even pay Jack and Diane a management fee.

Jack and Diane own 100% of a business valued at $1 million. If they give 20% of the shares to their children, that gift probably should not be valued at $200,000 because an independent buyer is not likely to pay that much for a 20% share in a family company. A discount of, say, 25% ($50,000) might be claimed, valuing the transfer at $150,000.

A Family Limited Partnership may help to increase the size of such valuation discounts. In the above example, if Jack and Diane received gifts of shares outright they could sell them to a willing buyer at a given price. On the other hand, if they received Family Limited Partnership interests and the fractional interest were held within the partnership, Jack and Diane might not be able to transfer their interest without the general partner's consent. Even if that consent were available, a buyer probably would be less interested in acquiring limited partnership interest than in buying the shares outright.

The bottom line: a Family Limited Partnership might enable you to transfer $2 million worth of assets to your children while incurring a taxable gift of only $1.5 million, $1.2 million, or even $1 million. Valuation discounts may be available even on transfer of publicly traded securities. A recent court case confirmed a valuation discount of 40% on a partnership funded solely with marketable securities.

Recently the IRS has indicated it will look hard at valuation discounts claimed by Family Limited Partnerships. As of July 1998, 14% of all gift and estate tax returns under examination involved Family Limited Partnerships, The Wall Street Journal reported.

Therefore, all the formalities should be followed closely. A genuine partnership must be formed and there should be a separate bank account for the partnership along with correspondence among the partners referring to the partnership's existence. In addition, there should be other reasons for forming a Family Limited Partnership besides tax avoidance. Those reasons should be set out in the partnership agreement. A few reasons for the creation of a Family Limited Partnership are asset protection, centralized management of investment real estate, a desire to keep a portfolio of marketable securities intact, volume discounts on portfolio management fees, aid for family members who are incapable of managing their own assets, and avoidance of conflicts among family members. To avoid adverse consequences on audit, respect the entity.

THE WEALTH TRUST®

John and Mary Smith's story shows how The Wealth Trust® can serve as an emergency retirement plan. John is a successful business owner who transferred some of his wealth to his wife Mary who used $650,000 (the exemption in effect at the time) to fund a Personal Access Wealth Trust and named John as trustee. Their children and grandchildren are named as beneficiaries, along with John.

John, as trustee, can distribute trust assets to any of the beneficiaries, including himself. If such distributions are required by the trust documents to be for "health, education, maintenance and support," the trust assets will not be included in John's taxable estate. In practice, virtually any important need can be covered by those four words. John can distribute funds to himself if they are needed quite liberally.

Therefore, you can serve as the trustee of your spouse's Personal Access Wealth Trust. However, if you are the grantor you should not be the trustee also because the IRS and creditors may assert that trust assets really belong to you. In many cases, you would name a child as trustee or your children as co-trustees. Your grandchildren can be designated as successor trustees, after your children no longer are able to serve.

Another approach is to name a close family friend, a personal adviser, or a relative as trustee. Such trustees need to be paid but they may be able to arbitrate family disputes. Your first concern should be to name a friendly trustee who will be sympathetic to the needs of the trust beneficiaries. Normally, the trustee should be able to distribute trust income (and principal, in some circumstances) to the trust beneficiaries, at the trustee's discretion. In addition, to make a regular irrevocable trust into a Wealth Trust, two powers should be added. First, include a provision enabling the trustee to buy and hold residential real estate. And give the trustee the discretionary power – but not the obligation – to let the beneficiaries use the trust property or properties.

Second, add a provision enabling the trustee, with the consent of the beneficiaries, to make distributions to pay the premiums for life insurance covering your children or grandchildren, which might come in handy if your heirs leave taxable estates or become incapacitated.

LIFE INSURANCE ADVANTAGE

Michael White and Anthony Thomas both decide to fund a Wealth Trust® for their heirs.

Michael's trust is funded utilizing growth stocks. Each year he transfers $50,000 to the trust that the trustee invests in the stock market. After three years and $150,000 worth of investments, the trust might own a portfolio worth $200,000 including appreciation. However, if Michael dies then the trust will have only $200,000 to provide for his loved ones.

On the other hand, Anthony decides to use life insurance to fund his Wealth Trust. He, too, transfers $50,000 per year to the trust that the trustee uses to pay premiums on a $2 million policy. If Anthony dies after three years, the trust will receive $2 million in death benefits.

In this example, Michael's trust won't even have $200,000 to distribute. The trustee will have to sell shares in order to raise cash for distributions and each sale of appreciated stock will trigger a capital gains tax.

Assume a 22% capital gains tax rate, including state and federal tax. Michael has a $50,000 capital gain (he invested $150,000 and the stocks are now worth $200,000), so $12,500 in tax would be due. The assets in the trust really are worth $187,500, after tax.

By contrast, life insurance death benefits aren't subject to income tax, in most cases. Therefore, The Wealth Trust® that Anthony funds with life insurance will have a full $2 million, after tax.

This advantage holds up even if they both live for at least 10 years. Assume that Michael's $500,000 stock market investment grows to $2 million, inside the trust, while Anthony's $500,000 in total premiums is enough to pay in full for a $2 million insurance policy; Michael's investment will still have a required tax on the gain and his after tax amount in The Wealth Trust® will be $1.625 million while there will be no tax on Anthony's investment in his Wealth Trust and the trust will receive $2 million.

That's why life insurance is a popular choice for funding The Wealth Trust®. Think of the money in your Wealth Trust as the last money you will want to use – you and your family will prefer to maximize the tax-favored growth. However, in case of an emergency, the trustee can distribute funds to the trust beneficiaries, who are also family members. No other strategy is nearly as powerful when it comes to providing long-term security for your loved ones.

THE ESTATE FREEZE

To see how an Estate Freeze might work consider the example of Ryan and Heather Davis, who are in their mid-70s with four children and five grandchildren. Not only do they want to minimize estate taxes, they are extremely interested in privacy and keeping their holdings confidential.

By 2004, Ryan and Heather had utilized their $2 million-per-couple lifetime exemption by giving assets to their children. In addition, they had been giving $22,000 per year to each of their children and grandchildren.

Next Ryan and Heather implemented the Estate Freeze Strategy. First, they established a Family Limited Partnership and placed $1 million worth of assets on the general partnership side. Ryan is the general partner and in control of the Family Limited Partnership.

Then they placed $10 million worth of assets on the limited partnership side with Ryan and Heather as the limited partners. Up to this point, no taxes were due.

The next step was to establish a Wealth Trust as a "grantor trust" – a trust where the grantor is responsible for the income taxes but the trust assets are out of the grantor's taxable estate.

The Wealth Trust® purchased the limited partnership shares of the partnership that held $10 million of securities. This purchase was structured using an interest-bearing balloon payment note. In order for such a sale to be recognized, The Wealth Trust® must be a "trust of substance."

To make their Wealth Trust a trust of substance, Ryan and Heather gave $500,000 in cash to the trust, incurring a $200,000 gift tax. In addition, they made sure that the generation-skipping provisions were met by subtracting the $500,000 gift from the $2,060,000 generation-skipping tax (GST) exemption that each married couple has. With the $500,000, their Wealth Trust purchased $7 million worth of second-to-die life insurance on Ryan and Heather.

Now, their Wealth Trust had substance so it was able to purchase the $10 million limited partnership interest. Because the general partner controls the limited partnership, the sale of the limited partnership shares were discounted by 30%, resulting in a $7 million purchase price. Thus, for a $7 million note The Wealth Trust®, was able to purchase the limited partnership interest that held $10 million (net asset value) worth of assets.

What's more, the $7 million note effectively held by Ryan and Heather is frozen: it will never increase in value even if the $10 million worth of assets in their Wealth Trust appreciates.

As a result, Ryan and Heather have removed $3 million worth of assets from their estate. Should Ryan or Heather live long enough for the $10 million of assets to double to $20 million, they will have removed $13 million from their estate, for a $200,000 gift tax payment. What's more, The Wealth Trust® now holds $7 million worth of insurance on Ryan and Heather's lives. After Ryan and Heather die, the $7 million of life insurance will pay off the $7 million note.

In the meantime Ryan, as the general partner, will use income and/or sell off enough assets each year to pay the interest on the note after paying capital gains tax. Because the trust is a grantor trust, the income should be taxable to Ryan and Heather as primarily long-term capital gain, taxed at 15%. If the income had been taxable to the trust the tax rate would be 39.6%.

The Wealth Trust® that holds this growing portfolio can stay in existence for three generations in the state where Ryan and Heather live. Later, it can be transferred to a state that permits perpetual trusts so it can last as long as future beneficiaries wish.

Thus, the millions of dollars in their Wealth Trust can stay in the family for at least 100 years and maybe up to 1000 years. The Wealth Trust® can subdivide in the future, for easier management. The net result is that Ryan and Heather have cut millions from their estate tax bill and arranged their affairs so that those millions benefit their descendants for generations to come.

S CORPORATIONS

Bill and Marie Williams are married, the only shareholders in Williams Corporation, an S corporation. In 2002, Williams Corporation earned $450,000 all of which is paid to Bill as salary and bonus.

To cut taxes, Bill could pay himself a $100,000 salary as long as he can demonstrate that it is comparable to the earnings of other top executives at similar companies. The other $350,000 would be considered corporate earnings, taxable to Bill and Marie on their joint tax return. Moreover, shifting $350,000 from earned to unearned income would save on FICA, social security and Medicare taxes.

Shifting shares in the company to their two children could have accomplished even better results. Between them, Bill and Marie can transfer up to $22,000 worth of shares each year to each child, without incurring any gift tax. Using discounts for illiquidity and lack of control, when they transfer minority interests they can make relatively large gifts.

Say that the Williams Corporation has 1 million shares outstanding and is valued at $1 million. If they want to transfer $22,000 worth of shares to their son Ted, they might say that each share is worth $1 and transfer 22,000 shares. However, 20,000 shares (2% of the outstanding shares) really aren't worth $22,000 (2% of the company). No outsider would pay that much considering the lack of a voice in corporate policy and the uncertainty of finding a buyer for the closely held shares.

Therefore, Bill and Marie can hire an appraiser who might say that 30,000 shares would be worth $22,000 to an outsider. If so, they can give Ted 30,000 shares. By using this strategy, they might succeed in giving Ted and his sister Paula a total of $300,000 in 5 years.

Now, the children will own 30% of the company. In that case, if the Williams Corporation shows a $350,000 corporate profit, $105,000 (30%) will be income to Ted and Paula. If the children are in a 25% tax bracket, rather than the 35% Bill and Marie pay on a joint return, that is an income tax saving of over $12,000.

In many states, income tax savings would be even greater. Moreover, the income tax savings are in addition to the payroll tax savings described above.

S corporation earnings are considered unearned income. Children under age 14 can have only $1,600 worth of favorably taxed unearned income per year (in 2004); larger amounts are taxed at the parent's rates. Thus, this strategy will have the greatest payoff after your children reach 14 years of age.

In the above example Bill and Marie still control the Williams Corporation with 70% of the shares. Thus, they can decide how much – if any – of the corporate earnings to distribute to shareholders and how much to keep in the corporation. Income tax will be owed regardless of whether dividends are distributed.

Transferring S corporation shares to your children will have estate tax advantages too. Bill and Marie have removed 30% of the corporation's value from their taxable estate without incurring any gift tax. You may not have to make a choice between an S or a C corporation. Often business owners have more than one corporation, C and S. They even can have some business operated as a sole proprietorship for purposes such as paying deductible wages to their children.

CHARITABLE REMAINDER UNI-TRUSTS

Case Study #1

Scott and Kelly live in California, are in their early 70s, and have an estate worth approximately $2 million. Many years ago Scott and Kelly purchased an apartment building that is now fully paid for and has appreciated substantially to a value of $800,000. Although the apartment building still produces a positive cash flow of $30,000 per year, Scott and Kelly are tired of managing the property and are also disappointed that they can no longer shelter part of their cash flow for income tax purposes since they have taken all of the depreciation write-offs that they are entitled to.

Scott and Kelly would like to sell the apartment building now, but have been advised that approximately 35% must go toward the payment of federal and state capital gains taxes. Also, they have been informed that even though their Living Trust will allow them to shelter $3 million free from federal estate taxes under current law, they will have to pay approximately 40% in estate taxes for their estate in excess of the $3 million. This means that their $800,000 apartment building, if sold, would only be worth around $300,000 to their children since more than 60% of the property's value would be lost in the form of taxes.

A Charitable Remainder Uni-Trust was the perfect solution for Scott and Kelly. Together, they formed an 8% payout Charitable Remainder Uni-Trust naming themselves as co-trustees. They also named an independent co-trustee for valuation purposes only, since real estate is deemed to be a hard-to-value asset by the IRS.

After giving the property to the trust and having the value established, Scott and Kelly, as trustees, sold the apartment for cash and paid no capital gains taxes. Thereafter, Scott and Kelly invested the full $800,000 in a balanced mutual fund that produced 5% per annum.

Although Scott and Kelly had other sources of retirement income and did not need the Charitable Remainder Uni-Trust income, they were delighted to receive more than $40,000 per year for the rest of their lifetimes, given current interest rate assumptions. Also, they were able to shelter a significant portion of the income over the next six years since they also received approximately $240,000 worth of charitable income tax deduction.

Although Scott and Kelly were very pleased with the lifetime benefits of the Charitable Remainder Uni-Trust, they had also planned to replace the value of the apartment building since they knew that charity, and not their children, would be ending up with all of the assets in the trust upon the survivor's death.

To remedy this situation, Scott and Kelly established a Wealth Trust. A Wealth Trust is a generation-skipping dynasty trust that avoids estate taxes for up to three generations. The Wealth Trust® also operates as an asset protection trust since it is designed to shield assets from creditors, judgments, malpractice and divorce.

Scott and Kelly named their children as co-trustees of their Wealth Trust and the children as trustees purchased $800,000 worth of second-to-die life insurance on their parents for a premium of $28,500 per year over a 10-year period, given current interest rate assumptions. Scott and Kelly, who had already doubled their current income that they received from the trust as compared with that received from the apartment building, were more than happy to gift $28,500 per year to the trust for payment of the life insurance policy.

Now, at the survivor's death, $800,000 worth of cash, both income tax-free and estate tax-free, would be in the trust for Scott and Kelly's children. Each child would be a trustee of his or her own separate trust containing one-half of the $800,000 or $400,000.

The combination of the Charitable Remainder Uni-Trust and The Wealth Trust® met a number of Scott and Kelly's goals. Together they increased retirement income, reduced current income tax liability, eliminated estate taxes on the sale of the apartment building, relieved them of the hassle of managing the apartment building and ensured that their children would receive at least as much as they would have had the apartment building been retained.

Case Study #2

Charlie and Marilyn are in their middle 60s and anticipate being in the maximum 48% federal estate tax bracket. Charlie, a physician, owns 100,000 shares of stock in a surgical company that he helped found.

The company's stock, which began trading publicly in the early 1980s, currently has a value of $30 per share. Charlie's tax basis in the stock is $1 per share. Because the surgical stock is a growth stock and the company reinvests all of its current earnings, it does not pay a dividend.

Charlie is planning on retiring either this year or next, and he and Marilyn are concerned about receiving adequate cash flow during retirement. They are also concerned about having a substantial amount of their wealth tied up in just one stock.

To meet their objectives, Charlie and Marilyn established a Charitable Remainder Uni-Trust and transferred 50,000 of the 100,000 shares of surgical company stock to the Charitable Remainder Uni-Trust.

Charlie and Marilyn named themselves as trustees, chose an annual payout of 8% of the trust's value for their joint lives, and named their own Private Family Foundation as beneficiary of the remainder interest.

Charlie and Marilyn are the officers and directors of their Private Family Foundation and are paid a salary for their efforts. The government requires that all Private Family Foundations distribute 5% of their principal each year to qualified charities. Their children, grandchildren and even great-grandchildren down through perpetuity, can also serve as the managers and directors of the Foundation.

Charlie and Marilyn, as co-trustees of the Charitable Remainder Uni-Trust, sold the surgical stock and invested the full $1.5 million with three renowned investment managers whose track records have exceeded 8% per year. Charlie and Marilyn will now be receiving retirement income of approximately $120,000 per year from the trust, where previously the surgical stock had generated little or no current income. Here also, they established a Wealth Trust naming their children as trustees. The children purchased a $1.5 million second-to-die life insurance policy on the lives of Charlie and Marilyn at a cost of $35,000 per year for a 10-year period, given current interest rate assumptions.

Once again, by using the combination of the Charitable Remainder Uni-Trust and a Wealth Trust, Charlie and Marilyn were able to increase their retirement income, diversify their investment risk, and increase the amount of wealth that would ultimately pass to their children.

Case Study #3

Jim and Beth, both 50, are physicians who plan to retire in 10 to 15 years. They have two children who will soon be entering college. Jim and Beth would like to establish a Charitable Remainder Uni-Trust as a supplemental retirement plan.

Although Jim and Beth do not own any highly appreciated assets, they do have substantial annual incomes between them and would like to utilize the tax advantages of a Charitable Remainder Uni-Trust net income with make-up provisions (NIMCRUT) to substantially increase their retirement funding.

Jim and Beth decide to establish a Charitable Remainder Uni-Trust with the net income make-up provision and to make contributions to the trust over a number of years. They plan to contribute less in the early years while they are paying for their children's college education, and increase their annual contributions after the children graduate.

The contributions to the trust would be invested in growth stocks and variable annuities that do not produce any current income. Since the Charitable Remainder Uni-Trust lacks current income, it will not have to make payouts to Jim and Beth until they wish to receive said income some time in the future.

When Jim and Beth retire, they will begin to withdraw income from the annuity that will start making 8% payouts plus make-up payments for the previous years when no income was withdrawn, giving Jim and Beth a larger retirement benefit for the rest of their lives.

The use of a Charitable Remainder Uni-Trust in this manner can be viewed as a substitute qualified plan as the contributions are not subject to the dollar limits that other qualified retirement plans are under, the trust is not subject to a maximum accumulation and/or distribution limit that applies to other types of qualified retirement plans, and Jim and Beth are able to receive current partial income tax deductions in the years contributions are made to the trust, thereby reducing their taxes on their substantial annual incomes. All of this is possible because of the net make-up income provision designed into their Charitable Remainder Uni-Trust.

MULTI-GENERATION IRA

Ray Jones, a 70 year old widower with a gross estate of $4 million and a $2 million IRA rollover from his former employer has named his two adult children as beneficiaries of his IRA.

Qualified Money Aggregated* Example: Mr. Ray Jones' IRA

Plan Balance	$	2,000,000
Balance Subject to U.S. Tax	$	2,000,000
U.S. Estate Tax (55%)	$	1,100,000
Balance Subject to IRD Tax (45.6%)	$	900,000
IRD Tax	$	410,400
Total All Taxes	$	1,510,000
Balance to Survivors	$	489,600
Percent to Survivors		24.5%

*Does not include state inheritance tax in excess of state credit, city and county taxes, or estate settlement costs.

If Ray was married and left the plan assets directly to his spouse, these taxes would not apply until her death. As you can see, the combined estate and income taxes can quickly erode the value of the plan assets passing to beneficiaries.

In August 1997, The Taxpayer Relief Act and Small Business Act became law and provided for the repeal of the 15% excess accumulation and distribution penalties. The removal of the excess accumulation penalty provides an opportunity to create a multi-generation IRA. To avoid the unpleasant consequences depicted above, and create a multi-generation IRA, several important decisions must be made prior to the "required beginning date" of the plan participant. Ray must select a designated beneficiary as well as a contingent beneficiary. Most commonly, the designated beneficiary is a spouse, with children and grandchildren as contingent beneficiaries. In the case of a plan participant who is single, the children or an irrevocable trust may be substituted as a designated beneficiary.

An excellent planning opportunity is available for a surviving spouse who elects to treat the deceased spouse's IRA rollover as his/her own or an individual who is single as of the required beginning date. Either prior to the "required beginning date" or upon receipt of the spousal rollover, one solution would be to name the children or grandchildren as designated beneficiaries.

When the plan participant or surviving spouse passes away, the value of the IRA account will be included in the estate subject to estate tax. If liquidating qualified plan assets pays the transfer taxes, the purpose of the multi-generation IRA is somewhat defeated. Also, this liquidation will incur income taxes, indicated in the previous example.

Estate liquidity may be created in several ways. First, the plan participant may systematically liquidate additional qualified plans and reinvest in non-qualified accounts within the estate. Another more cost-efficient method of providing liquidity would involve the use of a single life or survivorship life insurance contract designed to be payable upon the death of the plan participant. If there is sufficient liquidity to offset transfer taxes upon the death of the plan participant beneficiaries may continue to enjoy the benefits of tax deferred compounding over their lifetime.

Because of the leverage and the income tax favored treatment afforded life insurance products, often times this becomes a preferred alternative. Policies are typically owned by the participant's children or an irrevocable trust established for their benefit, and are purchased through annual gifts from the plan participant. If the trust established for this purpose contains dynasty provisions and includes grandchildren as beneficiaries, the plan may also create a multi-generation trust to complement the multi-generation IRA.

PENSION PHILANTHROPY

During a retirement plan owner's lifetime he/she should benefit significantly from deferred taxation accorded their qualified plan. However, the double tax burden of income and estate taxes imposed upon retirement assets transferred at his/her death may sadly deplete what the next generation receives.

Therefore, individuals with sizable retirement plans should consider stretching out the plan or consider making charitable entities their plan beneficiaries. Moreover, by utilizing a strategy such as a multi-generation IRA or charitable Remainder Uni-Trust, the plan owner can name heirs as the income beneficiaries, thus potentially increasing the net amount received by both heirs and their favorite charities.

The following example is based upon Dr. Leon Johnson, an 80 year old widower and owner of a $2 million IRA, who has a total estate of $5 million. Leon has two children ages 50 and 46, who are in the highest federal income tax bracket.

If Leon dies in 2004 and has named his children as his IRA beneficiaries, the following should occur:

Value of IRA:	$	2,000,000
Gross Estate:	$	5,000,000
Less Federal Estate Tax:	$	2,250,000
(Lifetime Credit)	$	555,800
Balance after Estate Taxes	$	3,305,800
Less Federal Income Tax:	$	413,297
Net Beneficiaries:	$	2,892,503

On the other hand, if Leon has named a Charitable Remainder Uni-Trust as his IRA beneficiary, and has designated his children as the CRT income beneficiaries, the following should occur:

Estate:	$	5,000,000
Value of IRA:	$	2,000,000
Charitable Tax Deduction:	$	323,160
Balance Estate to Heirs:	$	786,938
Balance to CRT:	$	2,000,000

Assuming that Leon's children receive a 6% payout from the CRT, based upon their joint life expectancies, they should receive an annual income of $120,000 for approximately 35 years, for a total of $4,200,000. If invested with a return of 6%, they should also receive annual income from the balance of the estate ($786,938) of approximately $47,000. Thus, their total annual income stream should equal $167,000. After the children's deaths, (and assuming a total growth of 6%) the charity should receive approximately $2 million.

If Leon's children simply received $2,250,000 outright, (as in the non-CRT example) they would enjoy an annual income stream of $135,000 (with a return of 6%). But by including a charitable entity in his plan, Leon will pass an additional annual $32,000 income to his children, while also giving a generous $2 million to his favorite charity.

PHILANTHROPIC POWER PLAY

A CRT, a Wealth Trust, and a Private Family Foundation can be combined to yield the ultimate philanthropic power play. For example:

Lance O'Brien and his wife Susan are each 60 years of age, and have an estate worth approximately $5,000,000. They have three children. Lance and Susan own a large block of publicly traded stock, currently valued at $2,000,000 that they accumulated as part of Lance's company bonus plan. Their cost basis is $500,000.

If Lance and Susan wish to sell their stock, they will pay $300,000 in capital gains taxes (assuming a 20% tax bracket), leaving $1.7 million for future investments. If they decide not to sell, their children could owe $1,100,000 in estate taxes (assuming a 55% estate tax rate) and be left with a $900,000 inheritance.

Instead, Lance and Susan create a Charitable Remainder Uni-Trust, to which they donate the $2,000,000 worth of stock. Acting as trustee, Lance sells the stock; because the trust is tax-exempt, no capital gains tax need be paid. Lance then reinvests the $2,000,000 in mutual funds yielding a 10% total rate of return. Lance and Susan elect to receive an 8% payout from the trust that will generate an income of $160,000 per year (approximately $102,400 after taxes assuming a 36% income tax rate). As the trust assets increase in value their income will increase proportionately. Lance and Susan also receive an income tax deduction, based upon the present value of the charitable remainder interest of approximately $82,000.

After Lance and Susan die, the $2,000,000 will go to the Lance and Susan O'Brien Private Family Foundation.

As required by law, the O'Brien Foundation's 5% charitable distribution obligation will be $100,000 per year. The Foundation can use the remaining $100,000 per year (assuming a 10% return to pay its expenses, including salaries to the directors (Lance and Susan's children).

In order to replace their children's inheritance that is "lost" through the creation of the CRT and Private Family Foundation, Lance and Susan establish a Wealth Trust naming their children as trustees and funding it with ten annual gifts of $36,315. The children, as trustees, buy $1.5 million worth of second-to-die insurance for a premium of approximately $36,315 per year over a ten-year period (given current interest rate assumptions).

If Lance and Susan each live to age 80, they will have received after-tax income from their CRT of approximately $2.5 million (assuming a 10% return on the mutual funds). They will have also made a $2 million donation to their Private Family Foundation that will greatly benefit their favorite charities.

Moreover, when Lance and Susan die their children will receive $1,500,000 tax free in life insurance benefits. The children will also receive continuing income as directors of the O'Brien Foundation.

LEGACY = LEVERAGE

Combining a Charitable Lead Uni-Trust with a Private Foundation enables the donor to reap tremendous estate and generation-skipping transfer tax savings while also making a significant philanthropic contribution. This strategic combination known as the Term of Years Foundation, allows the donor to leverage use of their lifetime exemption and generation-skipping transfer tax exemption on gifts to his/her grandchildren. This "leverage" occurs because estate tax liability is calculated based upon the present value of a future gift – the grandchildren do not receive the gift until the "term of years" (the period during which a Private Foundation enjoys use of the assets) has expired.

For example: Pursuant to the existing federal lifetime exemption any individual can shelter up to $1.5 million at death. That same individual can also transfer up to $1,030,000 in assets (in 2004) to their grandchildren (thereby "skipping" a generation) without paying an additional generation-skipping transfer tax of approximately 55%.

If Stanley Lafferty leaves his $5,000,000 estate to his grandchildren via his will, usage of his entire Lifetime Credit would still yield an estate tax liability of approximately $2,198,000.

Moreover, usage of his entire $1,060,000 generation-skipping transfer tax exemption would leave a generation-skipping transfer tax of approximately $980,100. Therefore, out of a $5,000,0000 bequest, the grandchildren would receive only $2,000,000.

On the other hand, Stanley could leave $5,000,000 to a Charitable Lead Uni-Trust for a term of 25 years, with the remainder to his grandchildren. Based upon several assumptions (including a 7% payout to the charitable beneficiary and anticipated growth of the assets at 7% per year), the present value of the remainder interest (the present value of what is left to the grandchildren) would be valued at approximately $942,450. By using the donor's $1,500,000 lifetime exemption estate taxes could be totally avoided.

Further, usage of Stanley's $1,030,000 generation-skipping transfer tax exemption would result in the imposition of no generation-skipping transfer taxes. At the end of the term of years, approximately $5,000,000 would transfer to the grandchildren, free of taxes.

Thus, under the terms of the above example, Stanley Lafferty can effectively leverage his lifetime exemption and generation-skipping transfer tax exemption to shelter the full $5,000,000 from taxes.

Even better, rather than allowing the government to take $3,189,100 from his estate (in the form of estate and generation-skipping transfer taxes, as in the above direct bequest example) he can instead leave roughly $8,750,000 (7% x $5,000,000 = $350,000 x 25 years = $8,750,000) to worthwhile charities!!!

BUSINESS SUCCESSION BONANZA

An ideal business plan will minimize transfer taxes, assure sufficient liquidity, provide for an orderly transition of control over management of the business, and safeguard the interests of both participating and non-participating family members. Combining a well drafted, well thought out plan with a Family Limited Partnership, a Wealth Trust, and survivorship life insurance, should allow you to reach these necessary goals.

For example: Dave and Julie Cunningham own several residential rental properties that they manage themselves. Currently, these properties are valued at $3,850,000. The Cunninghams (both age 55) would like their four children to have the opportunity to own and operate these properties one day. However, they face two problems. Their first problem is estate taxes. Even assuming that proper A/B trust provisions are implemented (thus sheltering $3,000,000 today from estate taxes), and assuming no growth on the value of the rental properties, after Dave and Julie die their children will owe federal estate taxes of approximately $450,000. Their second problem is that the children will have no liquidity with which to pay the taxes. Thus, they may be forced to liquidate some or even all of the properties to come up with the necessary cash. Fortunately, Dave and Julie can plan solutions for these problems.

First, the Cunninghams can establish a Family Limited Partnership and transfer their rental properties to the Partnership. The Cunninghams will divide the partnership into a 1% general partner interest and a 99% limited partnership interest. Initially they will own both the general and limited interests.

Next, Dave and Julie can gift 49.5% of the limited shares to The Wealth Trust®, established for the benefit of their children and even their future grandchildren. 49.5% represents $1,905,750 in underlying assets. However, the Cunninghams can make this gift to the trust without gift tax by allocating their lifetime credits.

Ordinarily, the lifetime credit can shelter up to $1 million in 2004 per couple for lifetime transfer of gift taxes. However, "discounts" on the value of the limited partnership shares actually gifted should be available, due to the lack of control and lack of marketability inherent in limited partnership interests.

Therefore, assuming application of a 35% discount as calculated by an independent appraisal firm, the Cunninghams can gift limited partnership units with a value of $1,250,000 that represent underlying assets with a value of approximately $1,923,077. This gifting should not trigger a tax or use the full $2 million exemption.

One or more of the Cunningham children can act as trustee of The Wealth Trust®. The trustee(s) can use cash flow generated by the 49.5% limited partnership interest to fund the purchase of a survivorship life insurance policy on Dave and Julie's lives. Premiums of approximately $20,484 per year for 11 years should support a death benefit of $1,000,000. After Dave and Julie have died, the $1,000,000 will be available to provide the children with liquidity necessary to keep the real estate assets intact. As a result of this planning, the estate tax calculations at the second death should look like this:

Rental Real Estate:	$	3,850,000
Less 49% Share Owned by Trust:	$	1,905,750
Balance:	$	1,944,250
Estate Tax at Second Death:	$	500,000
Balance:	$	1,374,912
Insurance Benefit:	$	1,000,000
Balance:	$	2,374,912
Plus Trust Owned % of FLP:	$	1,905,750
Net to Heirs:	$	4,280,662

Now, the Cunningham children can have the continuing opportunity to profit from the residential rental properties Dave and Julie worked so hard to establish. This is an excellent example of a Business Succession without planning that does not compromise the economic situation of the senior generation.